COMFORT
ONE
ANOTHER

LITERARY
CURRENTS
IN
BIBLICAL
INTERPRETATION

COMFORT ONE ANOTHER

---

reconstructing the rhetoric and audience of 1 Thessalonians

ABRAHAM SMITH

•

WESTMINSTER JOHN KNOX PRESS
Louisville, Kentucky

COMFORT ONE ANOTHER:
RECONSTRUCTING THE RHETORIC AND AUDIENCE OF 1 THESSALONIANS

© 1995 Abraham Smith

First edition

Published by Westminster John Knox Press,
Louisville, Kentucky

This book is printed on acid-free paper that meets the American National Standards Institute Z39.48 standard. ∞

PRINTED IN THE UNITED STATES OF AMERICA
2 4 6 8 9 7 5 3 1

Library of Congress Cataloging-in-Publication Data

Smith, Abraham, 1957–
    Comfort one another : reconstructing the rhetoric and audience of 1 Thessalonians / Abraham Smith. — 1st ed.
        p.   cm. — (Literary currents in biblical interpretation)
    Includes bibliographical references and index.
    ISBN 0-664-25178-1 (alk. paper)
    1. Bible. N.T. Thessalonians—Criticism, interpretation, etc.
    2. Bible. N.T. Thessalonians—Language, style.   I. Title.   II. Series.
BS2725.2.S65   1995
227'.8106—dc20   94-47642

In Memory of
Pauline Robinson Smith
and
Calvin Lewis Smith

CONTENTS

Series Preface 8
Preface 9

Introduction 13

1 · Charting a Course for Interpretation · 16

2 · Reconstructing Hellenistic Rhetoric · 25

3 · Determining the Genre · 42

4 · Reconstructing the Rhetoric · 61

5 · The Audience and Extra-Textual Evidence · 93

Conclusion 101

Notes 109
Bibliography 140
Indexes 154

SERIES
PREFACE

New currents in biblical interpretation are emerging. Questions about origins—authors, intentions, settings—and stages of composition are giving way to questions about the literary qualities of the Bible, the play of its language, the coherence of its final form, and the relations between text and readers.

Such literary criticism is rapidly acquiring sophistication as it learns from major developments in secular critical theory, especially in understanding the instability of language and the key role of readers in the production of meaning. Biblical critics are being called to recognize that a plurality of readings is an inevitable and legitimate consequence of the interpretive process. By the same token, interpreters are being challenged to take responsibility for the theological, social, and ethical implications of their readings.

Biblical interpretation is changing on the practical as well as the theoretical level. More readers, both inside and outside the academic guild, are discovering that the Bible in literary perspective can powerfully engage people's lives. Communities of faith where the Bible is foundational may find that literary criticism can make the Scripture accessible in a way that historical criticism seems unable to do.

Within these changes lie exciting opportunities for all who seek contemporary meaning in the ancient texts. The goal of the series is to encourage such change and such search, to breach the confines of traditional biblical criticism, and to open channels for new currents of interpretation.

—THE EDITORS

PREFACE

As the present study on the "audience" of 1 Thessalonians took shape, I became acutely aware that I was writing to *several audiences*—the classical specialist, the Pauline studies expert (especially of 1 Thessalonians), the biblical literary critic and *anyone with a fascination for literature*. The task has not been an easy one, and I am sure that my own appreciation of these various audiences will be enhanced by those who will read and review my efforts.

Four *contemporary audiences* deserve special commendation in helping me to bring this study to the light of day. Primary support came from a loving *philia* network of family and friends. I dedicate the book in memory of my mother, Pauline Robinson Smith, and my father, Calvin Lewis Smith. Neither lived long enough to see any of my published work; both still breathe on every page. Their children (Jeff, George, Mattie and Charlie) and grandchildren (Colin, Jamar, Keith, Ashley, Chassity and Cierra) are the only family I know, and because of the exigencies of writing, I have spent too many holidays away from their supportive ambience. Two nephews (Colin and Jamar) helped with bibliographical entries. Jamar, an avid mystery novel reader, fascinated me with his comprehensive knowledge of that genre. Conversations with him helped me to crystallize my introduction to Chapter Three, a study of a different genre, the one reflected in 1 Thessalonians. Not far from the Warrior River in Tuscaloosa, Alabama, one congregation (Pilgrim's Rest Baptist Church) nurtured my earliest graduate studies and my dissertation on 1 Thessalonians. Not far from the Charles River in Cambridge, another congregation (Union Baptist Church), prayed that this *completely new* work on 1 Thessalonians would *finally* come to life. I have found the best of friends and comfort from both.

Within the guild, several persons deserve special recognition. In all the good the book reflects, my doctoral advisor and friend, Mary Ann Tolbert, will see her influence. Vanderbilt University honored itself with her among its scholars. An inestimable debt is also owed to other teachers at Vanderbilt as well, especially Daniel Patte and Fernando Segovia. Many colleagues at the Interdenominational Theological Center and Boston University School of Theology aided my pursuit of the "audience" of 1 Thessalonians. I am especially grateful to the librarians of both institutions who indulged me in my meticulous research habits. Among the colleagues at Boston University, one treasured friend, J. Paul Sampley, read and re-read several chapters and offered critique and support when I lost direction. Yet, if there are any failures which remain in this work, they rest solely with me.

I live to teach and I have benefitted more from my students than they will ever know. Two students at Boston University, Mark Jefferson and John Dennis, read several parts of the text. John also gave valuable bibliographic assistance. Two others, Susan Travers and Andrew Irvine, completed the indexes. Andrew's careful reading saved me from many errors. I remain in their debt.

A word of thanks goes finally to another audience—the editors of *Literary Currents* and especially to David Gunn who shares with the Thessalonians an esteemed virtue—steadfastness (*hypomones*) of hope (1 Thess 1:3). *Grace to you and peace!*

—ABRAHAM SMITH

COMFORT
ONE
ANOTHER

INTRODUCTION

SIGNS OF THE TIMES

Since the most recent dawning of biblical social world studies, Pauline scholars have not ceased to probe the ancient remains for literary, cultural and historical clues about the everyday lives of the Pauline communities. Where the vagaries of time have left only faint traces, scholars have added "insights and models [drawn from other fields (social history, cultural anthropology, and the social sciences, to name a few)] to provide comparative material and theoretical understandings" (Borg 1988:284) to yield richer portraits of the "first urban Christians" (Meeks 1989). The old, strictly ideational explorations belong now to another age. A new frontier has seen the light of day.

Contributing to the quests for illuminating one of Paul's communities, the one at Thessalonica, are the recent studies of Robert Jewett and Abraham Malherbe. In *The Thessalonian Correspondence* (1986), Robert Jewett uses rhetorical criticism and social science to ascertain the profile of the Thessalonian church; and in *Paul and the Thessalonians* (1987), Abraham Malherbe uses social history and philological analysis to note how this early Pauline community was established, shaped and nurtured through the use of the Hellenistic pastoral care tradition.

To date, the two monographs represent the most disciplined and sustained interdisciplinary approaches to Paul's relations with the Thessalonians, and both works critically relate Paul's rhetoric or persuasive appeals to some exigence or situation creating the need for Paul's rhetoric to be written. In so doing, Jewett's and Malherbe's research informs the present investigation, and it is likely that all future inquiries on Paul and the Thessalonians will owe these scholars an immeasurable debt of gratitude for turning our attention to the social implications of

Paul's rhetoric. Their works are signs of the times, suggesting that we may not be too far away from the implicit wish of Burton Mack as cast in the following quote (1990:24):

> The move from rhetorical analysis to the social setting of a text is not yet a dominant feature of this scholarship. It is no doubt too soon to expect elaborate reconstructions of the social implications uncovered in the investigation of a rhetorical situation.

In line with the interdisciplinary approach of Jewett and Malherbe, the present study draws on a number of disciplines to explore Paul's strategic construction of the Thessalonians in accordance with a distinctive literary genre operative in Paul's time. I differ fundamentally from other scholars, including Jewett and Malherbe, however, in that I self-consciously raise two salient questions about the act of interpreting the profile of a Pauline community on the basis of Paul's persuasive appeals: *How do interpreters determine Paul's rhetorical image of a community?* and *What is the relationship between Paul's rhetorical image of a community and the community itself?*

To answer these questions, I begin with a chapter on interpretation. Because I want to look at interpretation self-consciously, serious questions are asked about the nature of the interpretive act, the interpreter's understanding of the roles of author, text and audience in the communicative act, and the validity of using a literary critical method of interpretation for investigating ancient texts. Chapter One will thus explore the advantages of using an audience-oriented literary critical approach, with which modern readers may join the ranks of Paul's "authorial audience," that is, a hypothetical construct of the audience Paul was likely to have had in mind when composing 1 Thessalonians.[1] If Chapter One is a reconstruction of interpretation, Chapter Two is a reconstruction of the authorial audience's view of rhetoric, its nature and uses. The chapter investigates Hellenistic rhetoric, that is, the rhetoric of Paul and his auditors, for the functions of rhetorical strategies in times far removed from our own. Chapter Three raises questions about the overall strategy of 1 Thessalonians. That is, the chapter determines which generic model adequately reflects Paul's overall strategic communication with the Thessalonians. With that generic model as the key interpretive constraint for modern interpreters, I then begin a protracted rhetorical analysis of 1 Thessalonians in Chapter Four. The chapter carefully explores the rhetorical exigence and the sequential development of Paul's argument in 1 Thessalonians. A fifth chapter relates how the image of the Thessalonians portrayed in Paul's strategic communication relates to extratextual cultural studies of the city and inhabitants of Thessalonica.

Not all is illumined by my investigation. I certainly make no claim to offer the definitive interpretation of Paul's rhetoric. Perhaps my contribution is but a faint light shining on a culture too deeply hidden in the dark corners of an ancient time for us to see. Yet, in the words of a recent interpreter of Cicero's rhetoric (Kirby 1990:xii): "I have thought it better to light the proverbial candle than to curse the darkness."

1

CHARTING
A
COURSE
FOR
INTERPRETATION

While general opinion may treat 1 Thessalonians as "dwarfed by such giants as the letters to the Romans, Corinthians, and Galatians," (Koester 1979:33) the letter's interpretation is far from a settled matter. One has only to look at current scholarship's varying positions on the letter's authenticity, its possible composite character,[1] and its relationship to 2 Thessalonians, to see how equivocal is the state of interpretation for Paul's earliest extant letter (see Richard 1991).

Differences in opinion about the letter are not confined to the current assessments of the letter. Ever since the 17th century work of Hugo Grotius (cf. Jewett 1986:3-4), scholars have registered their own interpretive opinions about the letter, with F. C. Baur and his famous Tübingen school being preeminent.[2]

Given these varying interpretations throughout the centuries, we initiate our study by discussing what constitutes a *valid interpretation* of a text, particularly of an ancient one. (In using the term valid, I mean convincing, not legitimate.) Chapter One then charts a clear path through the complex theoretical terrain of studies on the act of interpretation. Questions which the chapter raises and answers are: Can a text have more than one interpretation? Are there criteria for determining the validity of an interpretation? and Which methodology provides the best constraints for interpreting an ancient letter, if our goal is to know more about the contours and shape of the community to which the letter was sent? The chapter's aim, then, is to discuss the act of interpretation, especially the various pre-reading interpretive constraints which may illumine or even cast an obscuring shadow on contemporary interpretations of Paul's earliest letter.

The Possibility of Varying Interpretations

Interpreters of literature generally allow for the possibility of varying interpretations because of the limitations or constraints inherent in all three fundamental elements of communication, namely, the author, text and reader. While *authors* may not intend to write in an ambiguous fashion, they certainly have no control over the unconscious and unplanned formal and thematic connections which inhere in their writings (the "unplanned emerging into formal coherence"—Alter 1989:142). *Texts*, too, contribute to a myriad of interpretations, not least because of the heterogeneous elements of literature[3] and the indeterminate gaps in texts, whether the gaps are by design or not.[4] Likewise, the *readers'* inability to read texts in a detached or disinterested fashion also contributes to varying interpretations (Woodman and Powell 1992:210-211).

While all three of these factors in multiple interpretations could receive extended treatment, the most crucial for critical interpreters obviously is the set of constraints on the *readers*, for *all* critics are essentially *readers*. What is necessary, then, is both to note why *all* critical readers are constrained to read as biased or *interested* readers and to clarify the prevailing epistemological model that justifies a view of critical interpreters as biased readers.

One obvious reason why *all* critical readers read with biases is that critical readers of the past, whether near or remote, are subject to the constraints of explaining the past. Not to recontextualize a text is tantamount to leaving a text as it is, to ascribing to one's interpretation a lack of explanatory power and perhaps even cultural irrelevance (see Martindale 1991:46).

Another obvious reason why *all* critical readers read with

biases is that all critical interpreters, even those espousing apparently "natural" or "common sense" interpretations, are invariably influenced by, and react to, the cultural practices of their times (Woodman and Powell 1992:210-22).[5] That is, whether using an explicit reading model or not, and whether conscious of their valuations or not (Poulakos 1990), all critics strategically position themselves among their peers, whether predecessors or contemporaries (Fowler 1991:29). Yet, the distinctive advantage of any explicit model is that "it can be falsified" (Meeks 1983:5), that is, the model is readily available for scrutiny.

A basic justification for viewing critical interpreters as biased is the current intellectual acceptance of the social constitution of knowledge in all types of investigative practices, including scientific ones (Longino 1990:232).[6] This new epistemology or view of knowledge sounds a death knell to putative claims for pure, objective interpretation. The classical empiricist view of reading—a view which posits a passive receptive mind—is no longer in vogue, but has been replaced by an interactionist model.

Accordingly, all interpreters—critical or not—are assigned the fate of *interested* interpreters. Even early interpreters of ancient texts and historical figures were not disinterested interpreters. Aristotle was far closer in time to the ancient dramas and speeches than we are, and yet he critically re-contextualized them as distillations of actual practice in accordance with his own teleological system of probable actions as opposed to actual historical ones. And Luke, one of Paul's earliest interpreters, recontextualized Paul within a series of novelistic adventures (D. Edwards 1987; 1989:371-72) among socially prominent figures to dramatize the boldness (*parresia*) of Paul's Christian witness in impressive networks of power (Morrow 1982:434; Malherbe 1985:197).

While all readings are biased and while readers may vary in interpretations of texts, are *all* interpretations *equally cogent*? Certainly not! The current intellectual acceptance of the social constitution of knowledge need not lead one to resort to unbridled relativity or solipsistic readings without public, testable

18

grounds for interpretive validity. We chart below basic criteria which will steer readers between the dangerous Scylla of a monist and objectivist interpretation and the equally dangerous Charybdis of total meaninglessness.

Testing an Interpretation's Validity: Contemporary Criteria

While interpretations vary, and some are irreconcilably in conflict with one another, not all in the present age are convincing, some are better than others, and some are just plain ridiculous (Armstrong 1990:1). To make simultaneously the claim that texts allow for more than one valid reading but that not all readings are cogent ones, some criteria must be furnished that can test the validity of one interpretation vis-à-vis another. To assert that one cannot have a set of validating criteria seems disingenuous to me; the assertion is certainly not *any less political and disinterested* just because it is the opposite of what other scholars may think. And because all scholars are connected to interpretive communities, even that assertion is *actually* a type of criterion and it has validity itself with a group of scholars because they have so deemed it. Moreover, without stating clearly a set of criteria, a scholar actually gives license either to the critic who wants to say that his/her interpretation is the only definitive one or to the critic who in avowing solipsism interprets Paul's declaration of an imminent cosmic union (1 Thess 4:17) to be a reference to the "beaming up" of the fictional crew on Deep Space Nine.

Many contemporary literary theorists concerned with questions of cogency often posit three generally accepted principles as viable tests for valid textual interpretations.[7] The first principle is that the interpretation must not do violence to a text, either by ignoring some or all of its parts (Armstrong 1990:13; Sourvinou-Inwood 1989) or by suggesting that a text reflects modes of consciousness or social institutions which simply did not exist at an earlier period of time. When interpreters face anomalies, they must not quickly resort to interpolation theories, a virtual knee-flex reaction among a previous cadre of Pauline scholars, including scholars of 1 Thessalonians (see Jewett

1986:36-45). Rather, anomalies may help interpreters to read-just their interpretations in ways which account for the otherwise difficult features of a text (Armstrong 1990:25). Nor should interpreters resort to anachronistic views about Pauline literature which neither Paul nor his auditors could possibly have fathomed.[8] Indeed, one of the serious dilemmas of Pauline scholarship today is to get beyond the imposition of a bastion in Pauline interpretation, namely, the view of Romans 7:19ff as a recounting of Paul's introspective struggle. This view of Romans 7 has affected a wealth of scholarly lore, including Bible translations and existentialist interpretations of Paul's self-understanding (see Stendahl 1976:87, 94). Yet, the "introspective conscience" is a Western framework begun by Augustine and continued in the penitential piety of the late medieval church.[9] This framework, with its emphasis on soul-searching and despair before the coming of Christ, was anachronistically read onto a passage which essentially is a defense of the law (Johnson 1986:328), rather than a recounting of Paul's own life.

A second principle is that an interpretation must be communicated in an understandable and relevant fashion (Martindale 1991:46). This principle is particularly important for all historians of antiquity, including biblical critics, because the viability of biblical scholarship depends (as it always has since the allegorical interpretive period of the second century CE) on its ability to communicate in terms commensurate with the scholarly exposition of other texts in a given period of interpretation. This does not mean the *imposition* of a set of modernist or postmodernist values onto the psyche of a biblical character or writer. Yet an interpretation written to a modernist or postmodernist audience is *hardly finished* until one has critiqued the plusses and minuses of an ancient text's ideological framework in light of the current sensibilities shaped by the geopolitical shifts (Alter 1989:217) and changing intellectual paradigms of the intervening centuries. Indeed, Elizabeth Castelli's recent work (*Imitating Paul*) in this same series is meritorious among recent Pauline interpretations because it critiques the hierarchical ideology of ancient imitation, including Paul's, in light of contemporary sensibilities, not as a mere and simplistic denigration of the past but rather as a challenge to contemporary readers who would abstract transcendent principles and timeless truths from Paul's contingent and historically conditioned writings (Armstrong 1990:15).

A third principle is efficacy (Armstrong 1990:15). Interpretations which bring neither new insights nor new direction are hardly worth sharing. This is not to say that all previous interpretations must be cast aside and rendered useless. What is needed rather are interpretive studies which overcome the limitations of traditional, one-dimensional studies and add more effective analytical comprehension. In Pauline studies, Wayne Meeks' *First Urban Christians* (1983) and the interdisciplinary studies of Jewett (1986) and Malherbe (1987) do just that, for these studies investigate the wider social and cultural context of Paul's writings (see L. White 1986:63), and thus, they not only bring new insights to Pauline scholarship, but also they mitigate the traditional flaws of historical abstraction (Meeks 1983:2) and methodological docetism (the articulation of theological ideas with no concern for the structural forces precipitating them; see Best 1983:181; Scroggs 1980).

The present investigation rests solidly on these three validating criteria, for I propose 1) to consider 1 Thessalonians as an integral text; 2) to use a fresh and relevant interpretive approach; and 3) to investigate 1 Thessalonians in light of first century literary expectations. Yet, because different interpreters presuppose a different set of pre-reading interpretive constraints for reading a Pauline letter, a few words are in order about the methodological similarities and differences between my approach and that of Jewett and Malherbe.

The Present Interpretation: Methodology

Methodologically, my approach, like that of Jewett and Malherbe, is an audience-oriented approach. That is, I investigate Paul's rhetoric within the literary environment of an alien culture, and like them I seek to gain a sharper, less blurry picture of a Pauline community beyond the obscuring veil of the separating centuries. My approach, then, is not a traditional, formalist approach in orientation. A formalist approach equates rhetoric with style (see A. Smith 1989:48-50); limits interpretation to aesthetic appreciation; and fails to account for the strategic functions of a text as a type of argumentation "obtaining or reinforcing the adherence of the audience to some thesis, [or] assent" (Perelman 1979:10).

Yet, unlike Jewett and Malherbe, my approach is an *audience-oriented type of literary criticism*,[10] with attention given both to first century CE writers' exploitation of rhetorical strategies *and* to the limitations of ascertaining from these strategies the profiles and contours of a Pauline community. Thus, while both Jewett and Malherbe base their analysis of the social station of the Thessalonians on Paul's depiction of the Macedonians as "extremely poor" (2 Corinthians 8:2-4; cf. Jewett 1986: 120; Malherbe 1987:16-17), I contend that 2 Corinthians 8 has to be used cautiously and should be respected as a piece of rhetoric. As Wayne Meeks notes, the abysmal poverty of the Macedonians in 2 Corinthians "may partly be hyperbole occasioned by the structure of Paul's rhetoric in 2 Cor 8 which depends upon the antithesis of 'poverty' and 'wealth,' 'abundance' and 'lack,' leading on to the goal, beloved also by Hellenistic moralists, of 'equity' (*isotēs*, v. 14)" (Meeks 1983:66). Likewise, while Jewett (120) and Malherbe (16) allude to the "self-sufficient" references in 1 Thess 2:9-12 to suggest that Paul's audience was made up mostly of employees or of self-employed manual laborers,[11] I think a judgment about a correspondence between the rhetorical elements of a Pauline letter and the real conditions of a community can only be made after one has clarity about the functions of ancient rhetoric. Thus, my appeal in the present study is not merely that modern literary critics recognize the power of speakers to *characterize or construct* a rhetorical situation rather than simply *respond* to it.[12] I also contend that ancient rhetoric both revealed reality and "produced a response at the level of image and symbol" (Ober 1989:46), and one must first determine the function of various types of ancient strategic communication before relating the strategies to specific historical referents in Paul's world.

Thus the kind of audience-oriented approach used in this investigation has two distinctive goals. By initially apprising ourselves of the general rhetorical strategies of the first century CE, we *self-consciously* circumscribe the commonplace literary conventions with which 1 Thessalonians and other first century writings would have been composed as persuasive strategies. In so doing, we avoid the importation of an anachronistic literary consciousness or repertoire onto Paul and the authorial audience of 1 Thessalonians.

Moreover, by apprising ourselves of the genre of 1 Thessalonians, we clarify the specific strategic function of the writing and we limit the importation of certain critical pre-reading interpretive constraints which would have been unavailable to the work's authorial audience. To join our text's authorial audience, then, we may draw on the general literary and social repertoire available to all first century auditors and often exemplified by Acts and by all of Paul's letters. Yet, we cannot import the book of Acts as a pre-reading interpretive constraint onto 1 Thessalonians, for Acts—written much later—would not have been a part of the specific literary repertoire of either Paul or the specific authorial audience of 1 Thessalonians.[13] Likewise, we cannot hastily import critical pre-reading interpretive constraints drawn from Paul's other letters, though this practice has prevailed in much of Pauline scholarship in the past (see Sampley 1985:332). Our concern here is *not with Paul's thought* as critics may view it retrospectively on the basis of the entire Pauline corpus, or *with all of his audiences* for that matter, but rather with what the *authorial audience of 1 Thessalonians* could conceivably have known as determined both by the commonplace first century CE rhetorical strategies and the specific generic strategy of 1 Thessalonians.

Conclusion

This chapter has explored the methodological terrain of what constitutes a valid interpretation of 1 Thessalonians. While interpretations of 1 Thessalonians will continue to vary throughout the centuries, each generation can decide its own set of criteria for valid interpretations. Judged in light of the criteria chosen for this study, not all interpretations are valid, however, and many lead to conceptual bankruptcy and gross anachronism.

This study charts a different course and suggests that the best way to understand the particulars of Paul's rhetoric is to investigate the various strategies of communication operative in Paul's world. To begin this investigation, we first turn to an exploration of Hellenistic rhetoric. In so doing we may be able to reconstruct the "literary horizon" (Jauss 1982:22) of expectation shared by Paul and his reading publics. And moreover, we may be able to see that 1 Thessalonians, far from being a dwarf, has convincing ideas that loomed large in an ancient world steeped in the art of persuasion.

2

RECONSTRUCTING
HELLENISTIC
RHETORIC

Lincoln's Gettysburg address, an indisputably crafted work of art, may well be read apart from its literary milieu. So read, however, the speech is usually interpreted through the prism of 20th century interpretive constraints. That kind of reading actually says more about the literary tastes of modern audiences than it does about the auditors at Gettysburg or anywhere else in the United States in the nineteenth century.[1] Another way of reading the address, however, is to situate the text within its own literary horizon in the American Greek revival period of the nineteenth century, as Garry Wills' recent *Lincoln at Gettysburg* (1992) seeks to do.

In so doing, an interpreter captures the mood of the times, an era in which America defined itself in the likeness of ancient Greek democracies like Sparta and Athens (42). The address is read as a testament to the challenges of a President seeking both to inspire grieving mourners and to "refound" a nation in the image of ancient Greek democracies, democracies noted for their spirited public debates (46), popular or "vernacular speech,"[2] and majority rule (19). Moreover, the smaller constituent features of the speech—compact economy (149), antithetical style (55), "rebirth" diction (59, 78)—and even its larger funeral oration form (52)[3] are read against the canvas of a whole tradition of American authors, from Emerson to Melville, each of which advocated the idea of popular sovereignty (Railton 1991:19).

Likewise, 1 Thessalonians may be read apart from its distinctive literary milieu, as indeed has been the case in the neo-apocalyptic interpretations of the text in the past thirty years (see Jewett 1979). That reading is actually and perhaps merely a reading of our own habitus and a reflection of our own cultural assumptions. The goal of this study, however, is to examine the basic repertoires or pre-reading interpretive constraints available to ancient auditors.

Yet, reconstructing a literary horizon as distant as the one prevailing in Hellenistic culture is not an easy task.[4] Much of the literature of the Hellenistic world has been lost to the vagaries of time and even the retrievable data may represent only a modicum of the rhetorical conventions actually used in Paul's time. Moreover, the task requires some reconstruction of the cultural contours of antiquity as well, because literary conventions are actually cultural constructs reflecting the mood and spirit of a given period.[5] Without the cultural codes, we extract texts from their contemporary moorings and we run the risk of imposing our own assumptions and codes, particularly theological ones (see Stowers 1991:113), on the texts.[6] Thus to reconstruct Hellenistic rhetoric, the chapter begins by recapturing the mood of the times, that is, by articulating the impact of Hellenism, whether negatively or positively, in the Mediterranean basin and beyond. Then, the chapter explores three fundamentals of Hellenistic rhetoric by which Paul and his contemporaries moved and shaped the predispositions of their audiences: repetitive composition, exemplification, and *ethos* construction.

The Hellenistic World

Hellenism or the cultural expansionist policies initiated by Alexander and his successors in the fourth century BCE was both a bane and a blessing to the Mediterranean world for hundreds of years, even during Roman imperial times. Among Hellenism's negative consequences was the displacement of families to re-populated cities, a displacement which contributed to a sense of alienation and loneness as cultures mixed and many individuals were stripped away from the familiar cocoons of their traditional mores and belief systems. The increased travel of the period also played a dysphoric role in that it objectified the immensity and dangers of the universe. That is, the universe took on a transitory, insecure and fateful casting.[7] In response to the alienation and insecurity, then, individuals typically turned to astrology and magic (Garrett 1989:11-17), philosophy, or a variety of friendship associations (Jones 1964:21) for salvation, thaumaturgical protection or "mental imperturbability" (Fitzgerald 1988:52). Paul's congregation at Thessalonica made a similar turn (1:9), for Paul's personal and affective diction bespeaks a *philia* network (i.e., a friendship subculture based on mutual obligations, psychagogic support and moral edification; Meeks 1983:114).[8] Moreover, to assure his congregation of their ultimate security, Paul saturates his rhetoric with reminders of the congregation's salvation or deliverance from God's wrath despite the vicissitudes of the existing order (1 Thess 1:10;5:9).

Yet the Greeks' expansionist policies also had positive consequences. Because of the increased physical mobility initiated by Alexander and continued through several centuries of colonialization and urbanization (Meeks 1983:11), road and sea travel conditions were improved, thus making it possible for Paul and his contemporaries to sail up and down the Aegean or to travel along the Via Egnatia, the gateway between Rome and her Eastern colonies and the very road on which Paul made his ninety-mile trek from (the smaller, Macedonian agricultural center) Philippi to (the larger Macedonian capital city) Thessalonica (1 Thess 2:2; Meeks 1983:17-18, 45-47). And while Thessalonica was not an intellectual capital like Athens or an international city the size of Alexandria, its rank as "one of the two most important trading centers" (46) assures us that Paul found there the kind of cosmopolitanism and religious assimilation expected in any Hellenistic commercial city. For, in any commercial city of that age, a traveler would find the cultural exchange of ideas between the members of native and foreign cults, along with the predictable occurrence of family tensions and social alienation which follow conversions and shifts in "cultic arrangements" (Kloppenborg 1993:277).

And within the imperial power relations of the Hellenistic world,[9] the physical mobility of religious cults also became an important symbol of prestige for a religion and of power for the religion's deity. Whether the spreading of a religious cult was made possible through professional commerce, colonization or municipal business (Meeks 1983:18-19), the presence of the cult (and its shrines) throughout the *oikoumenē* helped the cult's adherents to "exhibit the universal significance of its deity" (D. Edwards 1989:366). The travel of heroes and heroines in the ancient popular literature, for example, became a dramatic medium displaying the power of a deity to vouchsafe the protagonists' fidelity and safety among successively greater networks of power (D. Edwards 1987:123). And Paul's geographical reference to "Macedonia and Achaia" in 1 Thess 1:8 is hardly an innocuous description of the people who have heard about the Thessalonians' conversion. Rather, the reference hyperbolically bespeaks the power of a god whose faithful and exemplary adherents are a part of a "loving" (*philia*) network larger than just the parochial spheres of the land of Israel.[10]

Yet another positive feature of Hellenism in the Mediterranean was the sustained use of a common language (*koinē* Greek—see Jones 1964:6; Bubenik 1989:302) and of common pedagogical practices, including the teaching of rhetoric. So, although rhetoric was initially taught as a part of the Greek *paideia* or cultural heritage,[11] the Romans themselves virtually adhered to Greek educational practices (Clarke 1953:11, 36). And whether in Greek or Roman times, eloquent speaking was a notable deference entitlement, for "the gifted rhetor significantly increased his or her social ranking" (Tolbert 1989:47; cf. Dio Chrysostom, *Orationes*, 24.3). Because of rhetoric's extended use in schools and even in popular arenas,[12] moreover, fundamental rhetorical techniques eventually became pervasive *throughout* the society. As a result, all writers, including letter-writers,[13] could *communicate and expect to be understood* in familiar and conventional ways, regardless of the literacy level of their auditors.

With a set of fundamental rhetorical techniques, then, Hellenistic authors steered audiences and reshaped events for their own persuasive purposes.[14] Of course, ever since the origins of rhetoric in the fifth century BCE Greek lawcourts of

28

Sicily and Leontini (Russell 1981:117), rhetoric was reputed to be a persuasive art with which an orator or writer could seduce souls (Plato, *Phaedrus*, 261A), excite fears (Aristotle, *Rhetoric*, 1.1.15), and selectively reconstruct events of the recent and remote past.[15] What the Hellenistic period brought then was simply the expansion and standardization of the art of rhetoric for all forms of communication (Brown 1992:39-40). Yet, to see how the art served persuasive purposes for Paul and his cultural contemporaries, we must now explore the fundamentals of persuasion in the Hellenistic world.

Fundamentals of Hellenistic Persuasion

An ancient writer or orator rarely related the *ordo* or historical order of events just as they occurred. Instead, through a *dispositio*,[16] a carefully crafted and yet formally variable presentation of the *ordo*, an orator or writer explained "occurrences in such a way that their bearing on decisions would be highlighted, emphasized . . . or given 'presence'" (O'Banion 1985:326; cf. Quintilian, 4.2.83-84). Emphasis today, of course, is easily effected through type setting cues—boldface, italics and paragraph indentation, to name a few (see Parunak 1981). In the continuous script format of all ancient Greek and Roman writing, however, other types of cues were necessary, both for basic organization and emphasis. Admittedly, deliberation on just three of these cues barely scratches the surface of what one could possibly say about Hellenistic persuasion,[17] but the following discussions at least reveal some of the fundamental ways of recasting reality to move ancient audiences from one predisposition to another. Moreover, these three cues, as we shall see in the chapters to follow, are especially significant in understanding Paul's generic and rhetorical strategies within 1 Thessalonians.

Repetitive Composition

"*Veni, vidi, vici*" (I came; I saw; I conquered)—these are the ruminations of Julius Caesar in 47 BCE after a sweeping two month campaign in Syria and eastern Anatolia. Indelibly etched in the annals of Western history, Caesar's epigrammatic lines are brief and balanced, compact and yet compendious. But they are more! They bespeak the character of a culture attuned to a type of speech which affects the ear.[18] Indeed, the Hellenistic world was marked by an aural and oral orientation (Achtemeier 1990; Parunak 1981; Tolbert 1989:107). All writing was vocalized; public or private readers read aloud; and *repetitive* oral compositional features provided signposts (Demetrius, *On Style*, 202) for the organization and amplification of an author's phrases, sentences and whole arguments (Welch 1981:8-15; Notopoulos 1951:100-101).[19] Moreover, the repetitive signposts steered the auditors, forcing them to follow the entire sequence, thematic development and intratextual associations of a writing.[20]

To some contemporary reading publics, ancient writers' seemingly incessant repetition occasions interpolation theories.[21] Others find Seneca's and Pliny's repetition aesthetically tasteless and monotonous, though the two statesmen were well-trained letter-writers (see Morford 1992:580). To ancient auditors, however, Seneca's symmetry and contrasts (Hijmans 1976: 98, 131-66) and Pliny the Elder's structured movement and parallelism (*Ep.*, 9.33; Gamberini 1983:181-89) added clarity and direction.[22] Moreover, in accordance with the descriptions and prescriptions of the rhetorical handbooks, even the repetitive patterns were occasionally interrupted by digressions[23] or varied with contrapuntal points[24] to alter the pace or shift the focus of a writing without forfeiting a writing's *synthesis* or organic unity.[25] In any case, the repetition and the digressions gave the auditors textually immanent markers for organizing and adequately perceiving what they heard or read.

Paul's request that 1 Thessalonians be read to all the members of his congregation (5:27) is a testament to the aural and oral orientation of the authorial audience of 1 Thessalonians. Furthermore, Paul's exploitation of conventional organizational forms—chiastic structure (4:15-17; Jeremias 1958:148); amplification (Stowers 1986:190, 206; Hermogenes, *On Invention*, 4.2); the transitional formulas in chapter 4;[26] and the abrupt, staccato-stacked maxims in chapter 5[27]—bespeaks his ability to control the pace of his letter and the perception of its auditors.

Exemplification

What the ancient writers could not emphasize with repetitive composition, they did with exemplification, the art of comparing or contrasting persons, places or situations with vivid examples. Examples were of extraordinary value to the ancient writers because of the wide range of "situations and actions, feelings and emotions" the examples could cover (Whitaker 1983:11).[28] Of course, for the modern interpreter, unequipped with the cultural literacy of the Hellenistic world (cf. Alter 1989:119), ancient exemplification is riddled with interpretive problems. Some examples were recounted in an inchoate fashion;[29] others were wholly or partially fabricated (Quintilian 5.11.6); and still others were based on the traditional diction of philosophical and political debate (M. Mitchell 1989:58-64; cf. Johnson 1989: 432). Any modern interpreter who surveys the examples in a quest for wholly reliable information then is hindered from the start.[30] Yet, what we do know about the *pervasiveness* and *functions* of exemplification suffices for understanding why it was a basic tool for Hellenistic persuasion.

Because exemplification vividly *amplified* an orator or writer's theses,[31] rhetors and writers exploited examples to add *clarity* to an argument. Before the Hellenistic period, Aristotle acknowledged the "easy intelligibility" of examples (*Problems*, 18.3);[32] later, the author of *Ad Herennium* (ca. 80 BCE) declared clarity to be the fundamental purpose of examples (4.35; 4.49.68); and still later, Seneca lauded examples for the precision or lucidity which they brought to precepts.[33]

Whether the ancient examples were parallel or antithetical,[34] "historical" or invented,[35] partial or complete,[36] manifested in polemical vice lists or exemplary virtue lists,[37] a number of Hellenistic literary genres (or forms) reveal, moreover, that exemplification also played a *moralizing or hortatory* role.[38] So, with antithetical examples, Plutarch guides the young ruler, Menemachus, toward a knowledge of ideal kingship (Fiore 1986:70; cf. 63-65). With a mixture of historical and legendary images of Socrates, Diogenes and Zeno, Epictetus illustrates the possibility of achieving true freedom (Donelson 1986:95-96). Seneca the Younger, with personal examples of his own strivings, exhorts "fellow-patients" in the cures of practical philosophy.[39] Juvenal, with tragic and comic stock models of the human quest for power, lampoons human *hybris* (Lawall 1958:25-31). And with allusions to exemplary characters from earlier narrative worlds,[40] even the romances, admittedly written for more popular audiences, advance moral identification with the virtues of their protagonists.

In 1 Thessalonians, Paul selects several apt examples to highlight the missionaries' or his congregation's endurance. In his self-description in 2:1-12, a description drawn with antithetical flourish, Paul lauds himself and the other missionaries as models of suffering forbearance.[41] The vice list (4:1-8; cf. Yarbrough 1985:81), prefaced by a request for the continuation of Paul's teachings, also plays a role in emphasizing the Thessalonians' endurance. That is, the vice list qualifies the holy and distinctive life which the Thessalonians are admonished to live continuously as they await the coming of their Lord.

Thus with the art of exemplification, Paul and other writers clarified their positions, moralized their writings and shaped the predisposition of their audiences in accordance with the constructed exigence or needs of the rhetorical situation. Hardly did it matter to the auditors that Epictetus' examples (Socrates, Diogenes and Zeno) included historical *and* legendary images. Nor did it matter that Paul's personal example (2:1-12) incorporated diction drawn from traditional philosophical rhetoric (Malherbe 1989:35-48). All that mattered was that the examples were *apt, familiar and persuasive!*

Ethos Construction

A concern for *ethos* did not begin in the Greco-Roman world with Aristotle, the rhetor whose *Rhetoric* lifted "this mode of persuasion to a parity with logical argument and emotional appeal" (North 1979:137). Instead, from Homer onward, one may trace the development of *ethos* as persuasive appeal.[42] Aristotle actually *limited* the *ethos* of a speaker to the work of art itself (*Rhetoric*, 1.2.4; cf. Ryan 1984:174),[43] though he must be credited with being the first Westerner to give a scientific examination of the function of *ethos* (May 1981:1). Only with

Cicero in the Hellenistic period, then, does a broader conception of *ethos* return, perhaps set into play both by the Romans' great respect for reputation and authority (May, 6) and by the prevalence of the "rhetoric of advocacy," that is, court speeches which turned a jury's attention away from the issues of a case toward a consideration of the character of the advocate, the litigant, the prosecutor and sometimes even the jury itself (May, 10; cf. Kennedy 1968:419-36).

Given this broader conception of *ethos* then, *ethos* construction surfaced in the Hellenistic world in at least two basic forms: 1) character embellishments (i.e., encomium and invective) and 2) typological characterization (i.e., the presentation of one or more characters in the scripted mold of a familiar, stereotypical persona). Both forms abounded and both were exploited by Hellenistic orators and writers to direct or block an audience's identification with the values of the various *dramatis personae* of a writing.

As for encomium and invective, these characterization forms originated in the West with the Homeric epics,[44] Athenian oratory and the dramas (North 1979:143-52). Later, the forms were featured in a variety of Hellenistic literary writings—moralizing essays and letters (C. Edwards 1993:24-28; Stowers 1986: 77), political propaganda, histories (Keitel 1984), rhetorical handbooks,[45] and the progymnasmata (or elementary exercises) of the schools.[46] Thus, it is fair to say that encomium and invective in the Hellenistic world had become standard fare.

In some instances, an orator offered encomium and invective simply and straightforwardly. In other instances, the delicacy of some rhetorical exigencies demanded a more subtle approach. So, rather than merely list a person's background, early development and achievements (Quintilian, 3.7.10-11; Hock and O'Neil 1986:101), the orator secured the audience's identification with or against a character's values by associating the figure with a familiar place or person[47] with whom the audience may have already had strong feelings.

In yet other cases, the orator could also focus on the praiseworthy or blameworthy *motives* of the *dramatis personae* to solidify the auditors' predisposition for or against a character

(Hall 1991:313-314). And where subtlety was not necessary, an orator could denigrate certain figures by beginning with a narration of the overwhelmingly virtuous disposition of other individuals before going on to narrate the vile and repugnant disposition of the principal characters (Theon, 107.19ff; Hermogenes, 9.24ff; Aphthonius, 32.27; see Bonner 1977:264).

In all cases, however, encomium and invective created a boundary between the orator and audience on the one hand and some supposed opponent on the other. Axiomatic was the care taken to castigate the ethnic, religious or philosophical background of the assumed nemesis *and* to omit or alter those facts which would lead the audience to identify with the values constructed for the opponent.[48] Occasionally, writers even denounced members of their own subcultures in order to delimit more narrowly the auditors' perceptions about the truly faithful or the truly moral.[49]

Just as standard was the practice of typological characterization. Tacitus' histories included a variety of stereotyped, fictitious or comedic characters (e.g., the informer and the victim) as models for real historical characters (Daitz 1960:31). But some writings exploited a stereotype based on actual, historical figures whose apparent idiosyncrasies made them easy targets for popular polemics. One such historical group subject to constant ridicule were the Epicureans. Because the Epicureans praised their friends, others castigated them as "assemblies of flatterers" (DeLacy 1941:56). Because the Epicureans did not believe that the gods controlled the universe, they were deemed as impious (51-52).[50] Because they advocated happiness, some thought they were hedonistic. Because they advocated otium (leisure) withdrawal, they were labeled as anti-social (52-53). Thus, while the group was an actual, historical group, what is said about them is a caricature of their true nature. By portraying a person as an Epicurean, however, an orator could summon before the minds of the audience the caricature, along with all of the negative emotions, feelings and antipathies linked with the popular stereotype.[51]

Occasionally, stock types were contrasted to each other to add vividness and clarity to a writer's character development.

Both Lucian the satirist and Epictetus the moral philosopher exploited a variation of "the wise-man vs. the tyrant" typology—a typological or stock antithesis contrasting the inner strength of a noble sage (philosopher) with the ostentatious and brute power of a tyrant (see Darr 1990:151-58; cf. Gray 1986; Toynbee 1944). A chorus of other ancient writers contrasted rustics to urbanites (Vasaly 1985), true philosophers to charlatans (Malherbe 1989:35-48), (faithful) friends to (chameleonic) flatterers (Marshall 1987:70-90), or any combination of the above.[52]

Just because an orator chose to use a combination of stereotypes, however, one must not assume that the *ethos* portrayals were presented in a haphazard fashion with little or no integration among the various caricatures cast before the auditors. Rather, as John Kirby has noted (1990:48-50), ancient auditors could expect a typological "web of *ethos*" or an ethical constellation center to which all of the *dramatis personae* would be linked. That is, the various stereotypes were deftly woven together with rhetorical craft in accordance with the overall designs and purposes of the particular orator or writer.

A knowledge of *ethos* construction brings clarity to several passages in 1 Thessalonians. Given the Gentile constitution of Paul's congregation,[53] his caustic remarks about the "passions" and "ignorance" of the Gentiles (4:5) appear disturbing, or at least, confusing. Yet, as we have seen, the denigration of an audience's ethnic group was a standard method of ancient invective. As we shall soon see, Paul's purpose here is to create boundaries around his nascent community, lest the church return to its former network of associations.[54]

Equally disturbing is the vituperative passage in 2:14-16. In fact, from the time of Ferdinand Baur in the 19th century to the present, scholars have doubted the authenticity of 2:14-16, especially because of its apparent anti-Jewish valence. Still, as Jon Weatherly's critique shows (1991), the evidence against including the verses, whether on formal, theological or linguistic grounds, is simply not extensive enough to "overcome the total lack of confirming textual evidence" (Hagner 1993:130-36).

The passage, however vitriolic against (some) Jews[55] is not historically unlikely for Paul to have written, especially when one reads the verses in light of ancient methods of embellishment and typological characterization, Paul's own rhetorical development and the implied anti-Gentile emphasis of the passage. As we have noted, ancient writers vilified members of their own ethnic communities, when doing so gave them a particular rhetorical advantage. How then does Paul's vilification of some Jews work to his rhetorical advantage? The early parts of the letter (1:1–2:12) almost overwhelm the audience with laudatory remarks about the congregation's *noble* ethos. After a brief orienting introduction (see further below, Chapter Four), Paul parades the exemplary faithfulness of the congregation, from the early moments of their founding to the present (1:6-10). Then, in the ancient typological register of friendship, Paul describes the noble character of the missionaries (2:1-12). Like true friends in that age, the missionaries are not flatterers (2:5);[56] nor do they *change* over time,[57] for whether as pedagogical nurse (2:8) or as pedagogical father (2:11), the missionaries have secured the maturation of the congregation.[58] Has Paul's self-description veered off the track of a laudation about the congregation? Not really! In the ancient conception of friendship, a person's character was often reflected in his or her associates (Saller 1982:109). Thus, Paul's winding remarks on the missionaries as true friends actually is a mimetic prism through which the Thessalonians may observe more about their own noble *ethos*.[59]

With 2:13-16, however, Paul makes a brilliant shift. What begins as a brief reiteration of the congregation's noble virtues (2:13) turns into a compact digression about the hindrances of the congregation's own countrymen (2:14-16). Yet, the digression is not without logic. It sets up a contrast between the congregation and its own countrymen. Although 2:14-16 is scripted as a vilification of some Jews, it is actually another *mimetic prism* through which the auditors may view both the dishonorable character of their own countrymen and, by inference, the more virtuous character of their own lives for having made the right responses to the truth (2:13). Thus, in effect, the vilification in 2:13-16 is actually a polemic against those Gentiles whose *hindrance* of the gospel stand in opposition to the *exemplary* suffering of the missionaries and the Thessalonians.

A knowledge of the art of *ethos* construction also gives clarity about the *rhetorical function* of the work/toil imagery in 2:1-12. Because the issue of the work/toil diction is of fundamental importance for this study's thesis, moreover, a protracted discussion is necessary. Typical discussions of 2:1-12 restrict the typological registers to "the true philosopher vs. the charlatan/flatterer" and the "friend vs. flatterer" antitheses (Malherbe 1970; Marshall 1987:310; cf. Dio Chrysostom, *Discourses*, 48.10). Yet, the greedy and pretentious flatterer was also the antithesis of the hardworking, independent and simple rustic. Edwin Ramage, who notes the prevalence of the typology, including its use by Greek and Latin authors (Menander, Plautus, Terence; see Ramage 1960:67; 1966), suggests that the overly sophisticated urbanite was often associated with flattery and sycophancy, as in the case of Sikon, the cook, in Menander's "Dyskolos" (ll. 487-498) where Sikon actually brags about his flattering abilities. In the same play, however, the young rustic, Gorgias, is lauded by the god Pan for practical wisdom ("the lad has sense beyond his age," l. 28) and philanthropy (ll. 682-85; cf. Ramage 1966:195, 200, 208-209). L. A. Post suggests that the whole play "conveys the impression that rustic life embodies an ancient ideal of equality, independence, tranquility and peace" (1960:160). Raffaella Cribiore also notes that elsewhere Menander's works celebrate rustic life as a place of peace, experiential wisdom and freedom from "the troubles of the agora" (1992:255). Ann Vasaly (1985:14) observes that Cicero also exploited "the urbanite vs. the rustic" typology in his *Pro Roscio* speech, despite the fact that elsewhere he joins his fellow aristocrats in vehemently castigating anyone who worked for a living (*Pro Flacco*, 18; *De Officiis*, 1.42). In *Pro Roscio*, Cicero lauded agricultural occupations, then, because in so doing he could prove that his client-defendant, Roscio, a rustic of sorts,[60] could not be guilty of parricide, an act which could only be committed—in Cicero's reckoning—by excessive (6), greedy (86) and shameless (118) city-dwellers (Vasaly 1985: 14).[61] Instead, Roscio is presented in the image of an admirable rustic—thrifty (75), wise (49) and modest (128, 143-44).

In 2:1-12, Paul's self-description contrasts the deception, cunning wit and flattery of typical marketplace speakers (2:3-5) with the hard work and toil (2:9) of the apostles.[62] By showing that the apostles chose the route of hard work and self-sufficiency, Paul demonstrates the virtue of the apostles, for in ancient times toil and self-sufficiency were conventionally regarded as demonstrations of virtuous character.[63] In portraying the missionaries' pedagogical philanthropy (2:9-12), moreover, Paul enhances the apostles' virtuous character, for selfless responsible modeling for others was also deemed to be an ancient ideal of virtue (Newman 1988:150-51). With city slickers cast as opponents (2:3, 4), then, the apostles are stereotyped as hard working, philanthropic rustics.

Of course, some scholars think that the expression "we worked night and day" (2:9) is a reference to the social profile of Paul, and by extension, of his congregation.[64] To support this contention, however, an interpreter would have to conflate several verses in the Pauline letters and in Acts: 1) 1 Thess 2:9, where Paul speaks about his work in Thessalonica; 2) 1 Cor 4: 12, where Paul insists that he toiled and worked with his own hands; 3) Acts 18:3, where Luke infers that Paul is a *skēnopoios*, that is, a "tentmaker" (or leatherworker; cf. Hock 1980:20-21); and 4) 1 Thess 4:11, where Paul tells his congregation to work with their own hands. The reasoning is as follows: If Paul as a leatherworker worked with his own hands, then the admonition to "work with your own hands" must be a specific reference to that trade.

Aside from the fact that this kind of argument depends, like a stack of cards, on Luke's rather laconic remarks about Paul's occupation, there are other problems as well. For one, as we have seen, the diction of toil in the ancient world was often associated with virtuous simplicity and independence. Some ancient writers viewed hard work as a condensation symbol for virtuous toil in the likeness of a Hercules.[65] And in his utopian reflections, Seneca contrasts the simple, hard-working life of the ancestors of Rome with the frenetic dispositions of his glory-seeking contemporaries.[66] In both 2:9 and 4:11, then, Paul's self-sufficiency references may well *only* indicate the virtuous character of Paul or his congregation. Second, the claim that the Thessalonians were all manual laborers restricts Paul's congregation to a monolithic group, an unlikely assumption given the heterogeneous constituency of religious traditions in the Greco-Roman world.[67] Third, the manual laborers hypothesis fails to account adequately for the similar toil and work diction found elsewhere in Paul's letter. Are Paul's introductory remarks (1:3) about "work" (ergou) and "labor" (kopou) indications of the congregation's artisan social profile? And later, when Paul acknowledges God's word to be "at work" (energeitai) in the community (2:13), does Paul here indicate God's involvement in the community's artisan work? As a "fellow-worker" (synergon) with God (3:2), does Timothy ply a trade with God? In 3:5, when Paul exposes his ruminations about the possibility of lost "labor" (kopos), can he mean his manual labor was susceptible to a loss? Or what is the interpreter to make of Paul's admonitions in 5:12-13? Are the Thessalonians to respect those who "toil over them" (kopiontas) and to esteem them highly for their manual work (ergon)?

A more convincing approach to the work and toil diction seems to be simply to see the language as Paul's integrated and coherent *construction* of his congregation. In an effort to demonstrate the *nature* of his congregation's prestige, Paul constructs an image of prestige that stresses interior qualities (work of faith, labor of love, steadfastness of hope, 1:3ff) rather than external opinions of the masses in Thessalonica. The self-description in 2:1-12, then, *functions* as a mimetic prism to clarify the virtuous character of the congregation's prestige. The missionaries did not seek glory from others (2:6). Yet, in hard work and toil, they demonstrated their virtue. For Paul, believers are called into God's glory (2:12), and they may boast eventually because of their virtuous aid in bringing others to maturity (2:19), but believers must not seek glory from men (2:5). To be sure, members of the congregation should esteem those who toil over them for their work of habituation (5:13), but this only means that acts of virtue are recognizable; it does not mean that virtuous people seek the recognition.[68] The challenge to "work with your own hands" (4:11) then is a challenge to the congregation to carve out their prestige through their exemplary independence. Like the missionaries who were earlier drawn in the typological register of simple, independent and hardworking rustics as opposed to flattering, dependent glory-seekers, the congregation is also drawn as simplistic rustics. Not only are they told to work with their own hands and to be dependent on no one (4:11), but they are also admonished paradoxically to "strive to live quietly" (*philotimeisthai hēsychazein*, 4:11; cf. Malherbe 1987:105). In ancient times, *philotimeisthai* was often used to describe a person ambitious for fame through the offer of beneficence to a community (Wardman 1974:116). Paul, with a rather wry twist, however, commends the ambition of "political quietism" (Hock 1980:46). Simplicity alone should be the congregation's goal, though to be sure, the very demonstration of their virtue will provide a fitting form for outsiders (4:12).

The picture Paul draws in 2:1-12, then, is one designed to persuade an ancient audience to understand prestige as toil and hard work for the habituation of other believers' growth; the picture is not given to provide exacting details about the congregation's social profile. As with Homer long before him, Paul lived and thought in a world keenly sensitive about images, and quite familiar with the *persuasive construction* of *ethos* through laudation and denigration or typological characterization. That these images were somewhat embellished and stereotypical rather than rigidly historical may be problematic for some modern interpreters, but for ancient auditors, the images significantly assisted audiences in *recognizing* an author's values and disposition.

Conclusion

More than a century has passed since Lincoln penned his Gettysburg address, and because of the great distance in time, a reconstruction of Lincoln's literary horizon is not an easy task. Yet, a whole tradition of nineteenth century literature is still available to yield a plausible reconstruction of the smaller constituent features of the speech, its larger funeral oration form and even the particular audience situation which made that form necessary. A much more arduous task, however, is the reconstruction of the literary horizon of 1 Thessalonians. With only a few remnants of an ancient past, we cannot fully illumine a culture deeply hidden in the dark corners of an ancient time. Yet, we have been able to see that Paul and his contemporaries shared a world brooding with fears, loneness and alienation. And when they spoke to those fears, they wrote in carefully crafted ways. They organized their writings with repetitive compositional cues to emphasize important matters and to invoke the active participation of their auditors. They also stocked their writings with vivid examples for the purposes of clarity and exhortation. Moreover, with character embellishments and type-casting, ancient writers predisposed and manipulated their audience to identify with the values of some individuals or groups rather than others. What we have not yet seen, however, is how Paul wove a variety of smaller constituent forms into a rich epistolary tapestry which would have been understood by the auditors of 1 Thessalonians. Nor have we seen how that epistolary tapestry holds together the threads of a specific tradition of literature, the details of which could help us better to understand the social and cultural context of relations between Paul and his auditors. The illumination of these unexplored areas becomes then the task of the next chapter.

3

DETERMINING
THE
GENRE

Traditional genre studies have focussed on formal elements. The more recent trend is to determine the *function* of a genre, that is, to ascertain a genre's ability to speak to the needs of an age, to answer its questions or to satisfy its longings (Hart 1986:292; Downey 1993:43).

So, for example, the popularity of detective fiction did not occur until the late nineteenth and early twentieth centuries because only then—and not in the time of Edgar Allan Poe,[1] the form's progenitor—did the Enlightenment's worship of reasoning and deductive detection gain popular appeal (Symons 1985: 21). Furthermore, Arthur Conan Doyle's detective novels (about the sleuth Sherlock Holmes), gained notoriety precisely because Doyle's fiction brought reassurance to the established hierarchical order of Victorian England at a time when English aristocrats feared the social unrest of the masses and the "rise of socialism and labor unions" (Clausen 1984:111).[2] Holmes' failure to question the basic economic assumptions of his society[3] bespeaks the conservativism of Holmes and Doyle and indirectly of Doyle's readership (113). Moreover, that the classic detective form evolved into the *anti-detective* novel—Umberto Eco's *The Name of the Rose* being a good example—is likely a testament to the persistence and adaptability of the crime genre and to the present postmodernist age, a time in which many writers no longer worship logic nor think that "a superior human intelligence can always resolve chaos into order" (Lock 1991:22).[4]

By turning the scope of this investigation to the question of the genre of 1 Thessalonians, then, we may be able to determine both the specific *function* of 1 Thessalonians and more specific information about Paul's auditors, their needs, questions and longings. Yet, since the present state of "genre" studies of several Pauline letters is a hotbed for disputes, a few methodological and conceptual considerations are initially in order.[5] With those considerations, then, we may more carefully explore a number of proposals for the overall generic strategy of 1 Thessalonians, that is, its overall function and appeal to an authorial audience.

METHODOLOGICAL AND CONCEPTUAL CONSIDERATIONS

Methodologically, the quest for the authorial audience of a Pauline letter could begin with a search for either its rhetorical genre (deliberative, forensic and epideictic)[6] or its epistolary/literary one,[7] for both genre types inherently reflect *typical forms of social interaction* as well as shared preunderstandings between authors and auditors. Rhetorical genres are defined "by means of social contexts and characteristic activities of speech within those contexts" (Stowers 1988:82; cf. C. Miller 1984:159), and epistolary genres also reflect "the literary typification of social situations where two or more people interacted" (Stowers, 79). Moreover, any type of genre, by definition, is a fluid set of expectations or shared preunderstandings between authors and auditors (Kimberling 1982:47; Burke 1953:124). The determination of a specific genre is potentially helpful, then, in deducing the auditors' "appetite" and expectations,[8] and in discovering the contours and shape of a selected authorial audience.

Yet, rhetorical genre studies will not likely prove beneficial in the actual determination of an audience's profile, in part because ancient rhetorical genres functioned as *broad* stylistic modes into which several literary genres were incorporated,[9] and in part because the general *topoi* associated with *one* comprehensive rhetorical genre could readily be subsumed as a smaller strategy within *another*. This is especially the case with

43

the epideictic rhetorical genre, for its broad "praise and blame" *topoi* were often coopted into the deliberative genre, particularly when present praiseworthy features of an audience's ethos served as the grounds for a proposed action in the future.[10]

With epistolary genres, however, the "typical situation" is narrowed, and while epistolary genres also share the *topoi* of *proxima genera*,[11] the reduction of the scope from comprehensive modes and *topoi* to more specific ones aids the interpreter in discerning a more nuanced configuration of the audience's situation. Thus, since the goal of this study is to determine that narrow, nuanced configuration, we will treat the epistolary genre of 1 Thessalonians, not the rhetorical one.[12]

Conceptually, the quest for the authorial audience of Pauline writing does not profit from rigid taxonomic understandings of literary genre, for such a prescriptive conception focuses too much on the formal conventional *topoi* of a text without considering the shared adherence and assumptions between Paul and an authorial audience. Moreover, the prescriptive approach often leads to *sui generis* and mixed (or complex) genre designations whenever the investigated text does not exactly fit all of the known formal features of a selected genre. From an audience-oriented perspective, however, a *sui generis* genre designation is simply not possible because an audience would not understand a completely new genre (Tolbert 1989:50); and likewise, a mixed genre designation is virtually unnecessary because Hellenistic auditors fully expected writers to adjust the style and substance of their writings to suit the particular needs and exigencies of their audiences.

Adjustments in style and substance had always been a concern of Western rhetoric ever since the fifth and fourth centuries BCE, with the kairotic (or "opportune") theory of the Sophists (especially Isocrates) and the psychological speech theory of Aristotle (Kinneavy 1986:81-82, 88; Smith and Hyde 1991; cf. Plato's *Phaedrus*, 217B). Moreover, with the writing of *De Oratore*, Cicero precipitated the Hellenistic writer's preoccupation with propriety (Kinneavy).[13] Indeed, *De Oratore*'s systematic and moralistic expansion of decorum, Demetrius' emphasis on appropriate styles, Quintilian's discussions of expressive diction,

Longinus' stress on "timely" techniques and Horace's "sub-sumption of poetics in a model of social order" (Schell 1977: 32), all contributed to the development of strategies for "antici-pating, circumventing and co-opting audience predisposition in the service of persuasion" (C. Smith 1992: 76-78; cf. Hariman 1992).

Ancient auditors, then, could expect Cicero to alter episto-lary conventions or to add circumlocutions to his letters of recommendation so that his thought-felt recommendations could be distinguished from his more perfunctory kinds (Cotton 1985: 332). And likewise, Paul's various audiences could expect Paul to modify the *typical opening and closing formulas* of the Helle-nistic letter tradition, or even of a whole range of commonplac-es in-between, in order to meet the demands of particular exi-gencies and audience predispositions. Paul was neither obligat-ed to include the conventional health wish of the "typical" Hellenistic letter nor compelled to adhere strictly to a "thanks-giving formula" based on modern scholarly distillations from the Pauline homologoumena (Stowers 1986:21). And his letters re-flect a number of adjustments of *topoi* or commonplaces, de-pending on the needs of the exigence. Thus, if the aim is for Paul to check the growing factionalism stemming from the ar-rogant predisposition of some members within a community, Paul can use the philosophical diction of "irrational passion" (1 Cor 5 and 6), not to highlight the problems of acquiring a Cynic or Stoic version of personal freedom, but rather to dem-onstrate in graphic terms how *enslaved* the putatively *free* become whenever they operate their lives without a proper esti-mation of themselves or a concern for the community. Or if the exigence is occasioned by external force (threat, intimidation or some other pressure), Paul will readily resort to the "indiffer-ence" *topos* (Meeks 1990:334) not to help his congregations to depend on their inner strength but to inoculate themselves from the pressures, whether the pressures are experienced by a long established church like the one at Philippi, or by more nascent communities like those in Galatia and Thessalonica (Sampley 1991: 78, 80, 100).

Accordingly, our assessment of the genre of 1 Thessalonians

will not focus exclusively on the formal conventions of a selected epistolary genre, whether extrapolated from extant examples
or drawn from the meager sketches of letter "types" prescribed
in the Greco-Roman letter-writing manuals of Pseudo-Demetrius
and Pseudo-Libanius.[14] Rather, we will treat Paul's distinctive
cooptation of a *fluid* set of formal *topoi* as literary expressions
of a specific and *typical social interaction* between Paul and the
Thessalonians.

PREVIOUS GENERIC MODELS

In advancing arguments for a specific genre of 1 Thessalonians,
Wilhelm Wuellner (1986:7) and Robert Jewett (1986:103) assign
the letter to specific subgenres of the larger epideictic rhetorical
genre. For Wuellner, whose approach is formalist in orientation,
1 Thessalonians is a *paradoxon enkomion* (an oration which
praises the character of an individual even though that character is marked by opposing traits). While Wuellner gives no
specific examples of the type, it is not difficult to see encomiastic material in 1 Thessalonians, both because encomium
stands as the fountainhead for a stream of ancient genres
(epinicia, funeral orations, panegyrics, elegies, biographies and
romances—see Gentili 1988:111), and because Paul's laudation
of the Thessalonians is readily apparent in the early chapters of
1 Thessalonians (e.g., 1:9,10; 2:13; 3:6). For Jewett, whose
interpretation moves beyond Wuellner's strictly objectivist
approach, 1 Thessalonians is a letter of thanksgiving (71). Like
Wuellner, however, Jewett gives no specific examples of the
selected type, and both scholars select particular subgenres of
the epideictic mode because they regard 1 Thessalonians to be
laudatory in tone rather than admonitory. In fact, however, the
encomium and thanksgiving subgenres are not exclusively
laudatory.[15]

Abraham Malherbe's interesting proposal that 1 Thessalonians is a paraenetic letter has much to commend it (1989:49).
For one, it removes us from the handicap of earlier form critical
interpretations of the letter—interpretations which considered
paraenesis to be a set constitutive form within the "so-called
Pauline letter" without seeing how a paraenetic theme pervades

the entire letter. Likewise, it avoids earlier scholarship's rigid bifurcation between the earlier and later chapters of 1 Thessalonians (e.g., Schubert 1939:16-24; Bjerkelund 1967:134) by insisting that both the so-called autobiographical chapters (1-3) and the so-called admonitory chapters (4-5) were equally important for Paul's argument and equally paraenetic in style (cf. Stowers 1986:23). More positively, by listing specific examples of paraenetic letters and their *topoi* (use of paradigms, antithetical form, maxims and reminders), along with the history of the hortatory tradition, Malherbe provides interpreters with a broader social/cultural context of relations within which a glimpse of paraenetic letters as a transaction of a "typical social interaction" might be gained (1989:49).

Yet, there are problems with Malherbe's proposal. Many of the *topoi* he links to the paraenetic letter were not exclusive to that genre. Antithetical style spans a variety of literary genres and is characteristic of the Greek language as a whole (Alexiou 1974:151; Dover 1974:64); and the use of *exempla*, maxims and reminders also transcend particular genres (Mitchell 1989: 69).[16] Moreover, even if 1 Thessalonians reflects a paraenetic or hortatory style, one has to question whether the style is exploited instrumentally for a purpose other than paraenesis. Is the letter written merely to remind a congregation of what Paul has said before, or do the reminders and *sententiae* constitute philosophical, popular and rhetorical features which neutralize the congregation's present distress by directing its attention to its past successes and its special and distinctive knowledge of apparently self-evident truths?

A NEW GENRE PROPOSAL

In light of these questions and comments, there is then, a third epistolary model to consider, that is, the letter of consolation. While the letter of consolation was a notable form of psychagogy in the Greco-Roman world, it has received short shrift as a genre option for 1 Thessalonians.[17] To consider this option, then, we will initially explore the consolatory tradition, particularly in light of the pervasiveness of consolation visits and consolatory letters in antiquity.[18] Then, we will consider how this genre option can account for virtually every aspect of 1 Thessalonians.

CONSOLATION IN ANTIQUITY

The historian Gilbert Murray once described the Hellenistic Age as a period freighted with a "failure of nerve" (1955:119-65). And as we have already noted, the Hellenistic universe took on a transitory, unstable and fateful casting. Dislocation of families; radical and abrupt shifts in social relations; perennial political machinations in the Greek and Roman periods (Jones 1964:20); and the demise of the *polis* (at least in its classical form; Hadas 1958:20) and its institutions—all bequeathed to Hellenistic individuals a grave insecurity. Hellenistic individuals felt "helpless to control or influence the occurrence of misfortunes" and the misfortunes appeared "indifferent, if not hostile" (Martin and Phillips 1978:401). That specific means of consoling individuals would develop in that era then is not surprising.[19] Indeed, whole philosophies sprang up in the Hellenistic Age to teach individuals how to achieve happiness and personal freedom despite a variety of circumstances, including exigencies linked with grief.[20] Accordingly, our consideration of the means of bringing consolation in antiquity, whether with visits or with letters of consolation,[21] will bear heavily on philosophical writings— though, as we shall see, philosophers held no monopoly on the art.

Consolation Visits

Because the Greco-Roman philosopher was regarded as a moral physician,[22] able to diagnose and give prescriptive cures to the soul's distressful diseases,[23] he was readily summoned "to scenes of mishap and tragedy, where he was called upon to practice his profession as consoler . . ." (Gregg 1975:5-6). This is certainly the picture one gets when one observes Dio Chrysostom's assertion (*Oration*, 27.8-9):

> And if it is [a man's] misfortune to lose any one of his relatives, either his wife, or a child, or a brother, he asks the philosopher to come and speak words of comfort, as if he thought it were only then necessary to consider the future.

Visits of consolation in antiquity extended to popular levels as well. During the Jewish-Roman Wars, Josephus' visit to the town of Jotapata raised the spirits of a small Jewish resistance band, and when he proceeded to leave and get fresh supplies for the blockaded city, the people both urged him to stay and regarded his presence as their one "hope" (*elpis*) and sole "consolation" (*paramythian*). Using a third person reporting style, Josephus writes (*Jewish War*, 194):

> If he remained, they urged, he would be their one hope of the town being saved, and everyone, because he was with them, would put his heart into the struggle; were capture in store for them, even then he would be their one consolation.

And in a citation from Plutarch's *On Exile*, the popular character of certain consolation visits is duly acknowledged, even while caustically critiqued. To his exiled friend Menemachus of Sardis, Plutarch writes (*On Exile*, 1.599bB):

> For many people visit the unfortunate and talk to them, but their efforts do no good, or rather do harm. These people are like men unable to swim who try to rescue the drowning— they hug them close and help to drag them under. The language addressed to us by friends and real helpers should mitigate, not vindicate, what distresses (*lypountos*) us.

These few examples from antiquity help us begin to set in perspective the discussion of personal visits in 1 Thessalonians. Paul, himself, tried to go to the Thessalonians again and again (2:18), but he was not able to do so. Still longing to make a personal visit, he prayed that he might be directed to his nascent community in the near future (3:11). Until he could, however, he sent Timothy to console (*parakalesai*, 3:2) the Thessalonians in the midst of their afflictions. Timothy not only consoles the Thessalonians with his visit to them but he consoles Paul as well with the news he brings back to Paul on his return visit (3:6,7).

Consolation Letters

As with consolation visits, Greco-Roman letters of consolation also extended beyond the philosophical level. So, although the

49

Academic philosopher Crantor (335-275 BCE) is credited with the first letter of consolation, the consolatory tradition *actually* goes back at least as far as Homer.[24] And while all the philosophical schools and even the Cynic movement developed arguments for this tradition[25] or discussed consolation as a theme (e.g., Democritus' *On Those in Hades*, Plato's *Apology*, *Phaedo* and *Menexenus*; see Gregg 1975:6-9), the rhetors likewise played a role, for they converged their own stream of Academic reflections with those of the philosophers and of the aphorisms and maxims of folk wisdom (DeLacy and Einarson 1959:403; cf. Martin and Phillips 1978:403) to develop a "popular philosophy" of similar, eclectic commonplaces and historical examples as appropriate responses to external circumstances beyond human control (Fern 1941:205; Martin and Phillips, 407; Stowers 1986:142). Moreover, once the philosophical consolations had drawn their basic *structure* from the Greek public funeral oration, a genre structurally stratified by laudation (*epainos*) and consolation (*paramythia*),[26] the consolatory tradition then drew much of its *persuasive style* from rhetoric (so Cicero, *Tusculan Disputations*, 1.112-17), including rhetoric's moralizing *exempla*, its *encomiastic and invective embellishments*[27] and its *typecasting of dramatis personae*. So, in *Ad Marciam*, for example, when Seneca writes to end the protracted grief of Marcia over the death of her son Metilius, he *rhetorically* parades before Marcia a series of diverse *exempla* (of men and women, historical and legendary figures, personified and living characters; see Fern 1941:206), all of whom are models or anti-models of how Marcia should bring her grief—now three years in the running (1.7)—to an end. Beginning with the loftiest *encomium* and the most vituperative *invective*, Seneca contrasts his two key characters, the deceased senator, historian and father of Marcia, A. Cremutius Cordus, and L. Aelius Sejanus, a praetorian prefect. Then, once Seneca *typecasts* Cremutius with the sage-like virtues of personal freedom and self-control (1.2-4), and once Sejanus is drawn as a tyrannical opportunist (22.5-6) whose insatiable quest for power led to Cremutius' suicide death,[28] and to many a conviction and destruction of other innocent individuals, all the other *dramatis personae* are drawn from the contrasting images of these two principal figures (Manning 1981:11).

Moreover, although the letter of consolation began with Crantor's *Peri Pentous* (*On Grief*) and evolved to find its fullest and most memorable examples in Plutarch (*Consolatio ad Uxorem* [Plutarch's letter to his wife] and *Consolatio ad Apollonium*; Gregg 1975:24-26) and in the Roman consolatory letters and treatises of Cicero and Seneca,[29] it was also exploited by Roman playwrights (Ovid and Juvenal), Christian writers in the early Patristic period (e.g., Basil, Gregory of Nazianzus, Ambrose and Jerome, with Jerome writing at least ten letters of consolation [*Ep.*, 23, 39, 60, 66, 75, 77, 79, 108, 118, 127]) and by scores of others in the Middle Ages (Scourfield 1993:16, 24-25).

Thus, while a more careful examination of extant consolatory treatises and letters is forthcoming, this cursory sketch of consolation's literary heritage for now at least reveals why it is possible for different scholars to note the presence of a variety of *topoi* (both epideictic and deliberative, and both encomiastic and paraenetic) within 1 Thessalonians. The variety is possible because of the broad range of influences on ancient consolation.

The entire discussion of consolation visits and the literary tradition of consolation, moreover, reveals that consolation was a widespread concept in the Hellenistic world. Yet, we must not brashly force Paul's letter into a Procrustean mold. Instead, we must now counter possible arguments against the letter of consolation as the genre model for 1 Thessalonians and we must elucidate the common *typical social interactions* transacted by Paul and his fellow consolatory letter-writers.

1 THESSALONIANS AS A
LETTER OF CONSOLATION

Only a few scholars (Malherbe, Stowers, Martin and Phillips) have shown an interest in the conventions of a consolatory letter and none of these scholars asserts that all of 1 Thessalonians is consolatory.[30] Furthermore, some of these scholars are quick to point out that even 4:13-18, while a consolatory topos, is distinctive from any other consolatory section in Greco-Roman literature.[31] Of course, the same could be said for any non-Christian consolatory section as well.

The reluctance to see all of 1 Thessalonians as a consolatory letter is probably based on the letter's *apparent* lack of the formal structural units in a consolatory letter, namely, the "lament" (*sympatheia*) and the paraenesis (or the precepts against grief) (Stowers, 144). Such a contention is not plausible, however, because of three counter-arguments. *First,* other consolatory writers like Plutarch and Cicero (cf. *Tusculan Disputations,* 79), in accordance with Hellenistic rhetorical conventions, sought to fit the consolation to the particular situation, thus, avoiding "hackneyed consolations,"[32] and leaving "a wide margin for treatment and local color" (Fern 1941:7).[33]

Second, in letters of consolation, the formal lament section is often subdivided into a lament and a laudation, or other comments on how the misfortune came to the author's attention.[34] 1 Thess 1-3, in fact, is saturated with laudatory remarks about the Thessalonians' behavior during Paul's absence (e.g., 1:9, 10; 2:13; 3:6); and in the same three chapters, Paul recounts all the events which have taken place since he was with the community, particularly how he knew of their present state (3:16).

Third, some letters and treatises of consolation were influenced by other subspecies, and thus, they would not rigorously follow any formal *disposition.* As J. E. Atkinson (1985:869-71) has noted, for example, Seneca's *Ad Polybium* was influenced by the form and content of diatribal and panegyric letters.[35]

Of course, to demonstrate how the consolatory letter is a generic model for 1 Thessalonians, we must not rely solely on formal structural parallels, for our actual interest in the genre question lies in the assumptions shared between an author and auditors and reflected in the formal elements of the genre. Accordingly, we now need to demonstrate how Paul coopted the fluid set of formal *topoi* in the consolatory letter to express a *typical social interaction* practiced in the Hellenistic world.

Stanley Stowers notes three fundamental elements of *the typical social interaction* reflected in consolatory letters (144):

1. The writer may have a wide range of positive relationships with the recipient.
2. The recipient has experienced some major misfortune that is apt to produce grief.
3. The writer expresses his grief and provides reasons why the recipient should bear up under this grief.

As for the first element, most scholars would agree that 1 Thessalonians is full of philophronetic phrases (Meeks 1986:86; cf. Stowers, 60; Malherbe 1987:12; Johanson 1987:71), that is, phrases which dramatize the friendly and familial relations between Paul and his nascent community (Malherbe, 52, 74), both from his vantage point and theirs. Indeed, according to the conventions of friendship in that society, Paul and the Thessalonians are *obligated* not only to comfort each other in distress,[36] but to remember each other and to recall the comfort which each brings to the other as well.[37]

As for the second element, the experience of a major misfortune, at least two distresses are evident. The one most frequently mentioned by scholars (perhaps because of our own struggles with the question of mortality) is the Thessalonians' (existing? or potential?) grief over the death of loved ones (4:13f).[38] Yet, ancient consolatory writings were not restricted to sorrows over death. Juvenal's consolation parody (*Satire* 13) addresses the issue of fraud (Manning 1981:12). Seneca wrote *Ad Helviam* to his mother because he was exiled from her; and his 17th letter to Lucilius was written to console his friend against the impending dangers associated with a lawsuit. In his *Ad Brutum* (2.2), Cicero notes some letters his friends Brutus and Atticus wrote to him to console him because they were *separated from him*. Speaking of the variety of sorrows treated by the consolatory tradition, moreover, Cicero (*Tusculan Disputations*, 3.34.81) notes:

> For there are definite words of comfort habitually used in dealing with poverty, definite words in dealing with a life spent without obtaining office and fame; there are distinctly definite forms of discourse dealing with exile, ruin of country, slavery, infirmity, blindness, every accident upon which the term disaster can be fixed.[39]

Death then was not the only concern of ancient consolers.

Another distress, perhaps just as painful for the Thessalonians is Paul's *separation* from his community. Indeed, within the consolatory tradition, some forms of separation were equated with death (Nagle 1980:23, 35; cf. Cicero, *Ad. Fam.*, 1.3.1; Ovid, *Tristia*, 1.3). Moreover, the affective diction in 2:17-3:13—the shared longing of Paul and the Thessalonians to see each other (2:17; 3:6,10); the description of the separation as the experience of being "orphaned" (2:17, *aporphanisthentes*);[40] and Paul's depiction of his restlessness and resolve to get back to the Thessalonians (2:18; 3:11)—suggests that the separation, of whatever type, was a mutually heartbreaking experience. That Paul's orphanage so soon followed the warm reception by the Thessalonian congregation (1:9) adds to the immensity of the distress. And worse than that, who would expect the apostolic envoy and pedagogical father (and wet-nurse) of a congregation now to be an orphan?[41] The distress that the Thessalonian compatriots (cf. 2:14) have caused, then, defies even the most basic expectations of hospitality and piety!

As for the third element, Paul offers several consolatory commonplaces for why the community should not allow grief to overtake them. One stock argument is that "Others have had worse to bear and have behaved nobly" (Martin and Phillips 1978:403). In *Consolatio ad Apollonium*, for example, Plutarch (106B) speaks of Antimachus who "enumerated the misfortunes of the heroes and thus, made his own grief less by means of others' ills." The *exempla*, moreover, whether heroes (and heroines), benefactors or imperial figures, were often juxtaposed to anti-models who clearly had not behaved nobly. So, in *Ad Apollonium*, Plutarch admonishes Apollonius to imitate the noble (119D) who bear grief nobly and avoid those who have a spirit of weakness (116E). And, in *Ad Marciam*, Seneca lauds the moderation of Livia at the death of her son Drusus by contrasting Livia's heroic control over external circumstances to the whining and pining of Octavia at the death of her son Marcellus (3.3–5.6).[42] And 1 Thessalonians 1–3 is replete with *exempla*. On the one hand, Paul dramatizes how he and others (like Jesus and the churches of Judea) have suffered grave impieties and are noble examples already imitated by the Thessalonians (cf. 1:6;2:14). On the other hand, Paul has his list of anti-models as well. Certainly, the outsiders who grieve cannot be models (4:12). And the hypothetical sham philosophers who flatter others and tell people what they want to hear just for the sake of self-aggrandizement—they, too, cannot be models (2:1-12).[43]

Another stock argument is that the community must console itself just as it has consoled others. In Seneca's *Ad Helviam*, for example, Helvia is urged to find consolation in the other members of her family while Seneca was in exile.[44] And after the death of his daughter, Cicero wrote *himself* a letter of condolence (see *Tusculan Disputations*, 4.63). The Thessalonians, too, are admonished to continue to console each other just as they were already doing (cf. 5:14).[45]

Yet another typical argument is that death and persecution are inevitable and common to human beings (Martin and Phillips, 402). In his *Consolatio ad Apollonium*, Plutarch says (106C):

> So it is clear that he who tries to console a person in grief, and demonstrates that the calamity is one which is common to many. . . changes the opinion of the one in grief and gives him a similar conviction—that his calamity is really less than he supposed it to be.

Obviously Paul's apocalyptic framework predisposed him to see the inevitability of suffering (whether death or persecution) for the Thessalonian believers.[46] That much is evident in his recitation of foundational teachings about potential afflictions for the community (3:4).[47] Though Paul does not allude to death and persecution as the common lot of *all* humanity, the consolatory argument is likely still effective because Paul notes how even the most *revered* and *powerful* leaders of his salvationist religion had to face similar afflictions (1:6; 2:14-15). The sting of the Thessalonians' afflictions is removed, then, if they can see that theirs is not a singular experience of suffering.

A related commonplace is that suffering is a sign of a deity's approval, blessing or reward to exemplary individuals—not a sign of a deity's disfavor.[48] Of course, this enlightened view of suffering stood alongside the exact opposite opinion, that is, that suffering was "a punishment sent by the deity for past offenses" (Duff 1991:82).[49] In the logic of the enlightened view, however, exemplary individuals, like ideal sages, are *beloved* of the deity, as if the deity were a *father* or a *teacher* to them.[50] Moreover, exemplary individuals are *summoned* or *called* to be witnesses for the deity:[51] to serve as *models* or examples for the rest of humanity to imitate; to live *worthy*[52] lives as the offspring of the deity; to *prove, test and exercise*[53] their strength through *toil* and adversity.[54] As John Fitzgerald recently notes (1988:76), in Stoic circles in the Greco-Roman world, hardship was treated as a "benefaction bestowed out of the divine's love for humanity." Accordingly, Seneca's consolations laud toil (*Ad Marciam*, 16.1), constancy (*Ad Helviam*, 5.5) and tests of endurance (*Epistles*, 13:1-3; *Ad Marciam*, 5.5-6). The neo-Platonist Plutarch also viewed hardships—even death—as an indication of divine favor or love (*Ad Apollonium*, 111B;119E). Moreover, the concept of labor or toil as trials or periods of testing was so pervasive in the Roman period that one can see it in the high literature of Virgil's *Aeneid*[55] as well as in the popular literature of the ancient Greek novels.[56]

Whatever the source for Paul, the commonplace of viewing suffering as a test for exemplary individuals is evident in 1 Thessalonians. Paul's scattered descriptions of the Thessalonians as beloved (1:4), chosen (1:4), exemplary (1:7) and called (2:12; cf. 1:2; 5:24) are hardly innocuous tags. When not reduced to mild-mannered epithets, the attributes laud the Thessalonians as persons whose suffering, like his and others, is *indeed* an indication of God's love and approval, not an indication that they are candidates for God's wrath (cf.1:10; 2:16; 5:9).[57] The congregation's suffering is an agonistic workout for their progress and maturity. Viewing these laudatory remarks apart from reductionistic romantic lenses, we can see that the Thessalonians are admonished to understand themselves as children of a caring and nurturing father (1:1, 3; 3:13) or teacher (4:9). As such, they are challenged to continue to lead lives which are distinguished and holy (cf. 4:1-12), in effect, to be a veritable testimony to others on how to walk in a worthy (2:12) manner before God.

The most powerful commonplace argument for bearing up

under grief, however, is that of acknowledging an expected re-
union, a union which relativizes any present form of separation.
For example, in "A Pleasant Life Impossible," an argument
against the "atheism" of the Epicureans (see Stowers 1990:277),
Plutarch avers (1105E) that the Epicureans:

> do not think they will meet once more those friends them-
> selves, or ever again see a dear father or dear mother or
> perhaps a gentle wife, and have not even the hope (*elpis*) of
> such company and welcome that they possess who share the
> views of Pythagoras and Plato and Homer about the soul.[58]

For Paul, there is no need to grieve, for the parousia brings
the hope for a cosmic union, and this union, being so powerful,
overcomes both physical and mortal separation. Thus, this type
of argument explains how Paul can speak of his separation as
the experience of an "orphan" *aporphanisthentes* (2:17), and
almost in the same breath, he can relate the ultimate "joy"
(*chara*, 2:19) he will have at the parousia. For Paul, the parousia overcomes physical separation. It relativizes absence! The
event of the parousia also explains how Paul can speak about
the dead believers with such euphemistic terms as "those who
are asleep" [*koimomenon* (4:13); *koimēthentas* (4:15)] or as
"the dead in Christ" [*nekroi en christō* (4:16)].[59] The parousia
overcomes mortal separation to such an extent that it neces-
sitates a radical re-interpretation of the ordinary circumstance of
death. Indeed, it relativizes death!

In the case of Cicero, Seneca and Plutarch, all of the stock
commonplaces function to stabilize the recipients. In fact, when
Plutarch states that the goal of his consolation for his wife is for
her to become "well-stabilized" (*eustatheian*, 609D; cf. 611), he
is stating a cognate form of the very word "to stabilize" (*stērezai*,
3:2,13) which Paul repeats in his letter to the Thessalonians. For
Paul's contemporaries, however, the stabilization is achieved by
highlighting the *naturalness* of human vicissitudes. So, in *Ad
Marciam*, for example, Metilius' death is viewed as one of life's
many determined vicissitudes, not exacted without meaning, but
fully evolving out of divine reason; Marcia can thus bear up
with self-control because what has happened to her—the loss of
a loved one—*naturally* will happen to all human beings.[60] And

in Seneca's *Ad Helviam*, Seneca's otherwise heart-wrenching exile and separation from his mother is interpreted as a *natural* experience. As John Gahan explains (1985:145):

> Seneca develops at length the theme that most men are in a sense exiles (in that they grow up and leave home) and that confinement to Corsica is really one facet of a perfectly natural process of separation.

The goal of these consolers, then, is to provide their auditors with a hermeneutic based on reason through which they can maintain their personal freedom and equanimity in any and all circumstances (Manning 1981:11). Especially helpful in the philosopher's task of proffering a hermeneutic were specific philosophical precepts.[61] Sometimes couched in military imagery (*Ad Polybium*, 18.1; *Ad Helviam*, 17.5; 5.3; cf. Fern, 35), often formulated in gnomic expressions,[62] and frequently individuated or tailor-suited for special circumstances (see Malherbe 1990), these precepts functioned to aid the auditors in the habituation of proper attitudes and of a mental imperturbability toward the indifferent forces of the universe.[63]

Like the philosophers, Paul wants to provide his nascent community with a hermeneutic which stabilizes and secures them in any and all circumstances, for such is the sense of the gnomic precept "Be thankful in all things" (5:18), and evidently Paul dramatizes that hermeneutic himself by repeatedly giving thanks to God throughout the letter (1:2; 2:13ff; 3:7-9).[64] Like the philosophers, Paul describes stability with the military imagery of fortification. The auditors are given a picture of themselves as vigilant (5:6; cf. Seneca, *Ep.* 18.6; 59.7; *Vit. Beat.* 26.2) and well-armored soldiers (5:8; Seneca, *Const. Sap.* 19.3; cf. Tietze 1985:69), able to stabilize or build each other up (*oikodomeite*, 5:11) against any false judgments[65] about apparent security.[66] Unlike his contemporaries, however, Paul's *basic* prism for maintaining equanimity, as we have seen, is an apocalyptic hermeneutic.

Still, the foregoing analysis of a *typical social situation* reflected in 1 Thessalonians reveals that there are remarkable similarities between Paul's letter and the Hellenistic consolatory tradition—so much so that we can no longer limit Paul's consolatory goal to just one part of Paul's earliest extant letter, namely, 1 Thess 4:13-18. As we have seen, however, both 1 Thessalonians and the consolatory writings of Paul's contemporaries all share a similar situation, that is, the friendly presentation of consolatory examples and commonplaces to help the auditors overcome one or more experiences of grief.

CONCLUSION

Arthur Conan Doyle's classic detective fiction belongs to a long tradition of crime fiction with Edgar Allen Poe's "The Purloined Letter" as its literary antecedent and Umberto Eco's *The Name of the Rose* as a literary descendant. At the same time, however, Doyle's work satisfied the longings of a particular age, the Victorian Era, with its celebration of the scientific method and its rigid hierarchical values.

Likewise, Paul's earliest extant letter stands in the stream of a long tradition, the consolatory tradition—a stream that begins with Crantor's *Peri Pentous* and extends to the early church fathers (Jerome and Ambrose to name a few) and beyond. Within the Hellenistic Age, moreover, the consolation letter *functions* to restore individuals to a level of personal freedom and transcendence over constantly changing circumstances. Ancient consolation, so dependent as it was upon folk wisdom and stock arguments, usually spoke to the needs of Hellenistic individuals by giving them a broader interpretive context through which otherwise difficult events could be relativized (or understood). In the case of Paul's congregation at Thessalonica, 1 Thessalonians included many of the structural features and typical arguments found in the consolatory letter, though the principal hermeneutical context reflected in the letter was an apocalyptic one. With that overarching explanatory or rationalizing framework, Paul sought to help the Thessalonians to interpret present sufferings accurately and to prepare their minds for future crises.[67] Indeed, Paul did not expect the lot of the Christians to get any better (3:3), because he saw the Christians' suffering as part of an ongoing cosmic apocalyptic struggle. So, Paul attributes the cause of his absence from the community to *Satan* (2:18); and he sends Timothy to Thessalonica for fear that the *tempter* has tempted the Thessalonians and his work has been in vain (3:5). In Paul's interpretation of events, moreover, there is no peace and security (5:3)—no time when anyone can say: "Don't worry! Be happy!—and so, the community—like soldiers—must always stay on guard (5:4f); they must always remain alert (*Ad Helviam*, 5.3; Plutarch, *Ad Apollonium*, 119D). And although there is no question about their ultimate union (5:5-10), for now, the Thessalonian congregation can expect *anything* to happen—even the unexpected. The letter as well as Timothy's visit then are crucial in preparing the community with the mental imperturbability it needs while it awaits the cosmic unity. The letter reveals the proper responses the community must make to their circumstances and Timothy's visits model what the members of the community can do for each other until the parousia, that is, they can comfort one another!

Yet, more clarity about the crisis of the Thessalonians is in order. While the quest for Paul's overall strategy has elucidated some of the shared assumptions between Paul and his audience, a careful study of the rhetorical exigence, audience predisposition and the letter's argumentation will help us to see how the authorial audience would have processed the letter's organization and emphasis. That is, a focus on the rhetorical exigence and audience predisposition will likely reveal the motivation behind Paul's choice of consolatory rhetoric; and an examination of Paul's argumentation will likely reveal the sequential development of Paul's strategy for moving his audience from one predisposition to another. Thus, to pursue these goals, we now turn to the next chapter.

4

RECONSTRUCTING
THE
RHETORIC

Toni Morrison's third novel, *Song of Solomon* (1977), has hardly achieved the critical acclaim attributed to her later Pulitzer prize-winning novel *Beloved* (1987). Yet, the third novel is no less a work of exquisite rhetorical skill. Its anti-classical hero critique (Harris 1991:85-95), class analysis (Mbalia 1991:50-66), defamiliarization techniques[1] and hermeneutics of suspicion about senseless naming or "artificial symbolization" (T. Mason 1988:569) all render it an intriguing and unconventional mystery of undiminished aesthetic delight. Similarly, 1 Thessalonians has stood in the shadows of later works written by Paul. Until recently, 1 Thessalonians has had to wait in the wings while other Pauline letters had their day in the spotlight of critical exploration. The recent change in regard for Paul's earliest known letter is in no small part owed to a surge of critical interest in the artful rhetoric of 1 Thessalonians (Barclay 1993: 512). With this chapter, I assay to make a contribution to recent efforts to clarify Paul's adroit ability rhetorically to construct his audience and their situation. So, while the previous chapter revealed the overall generic strategy of 1 Thessalonians, it is now important to indicate how the smaller strategic units of 1 Thessalonians become visible for the modern interpreter, especially when we determine the sequential and dynamic compositional cues of Paul's argument in accordance with Paul's constructed rhetorical exigence[2] and the *dispositio* reflected in his choice of generic strategies.

Rhetorical Exigence and Dispositio

All exigencies depend on the constraints of the perceiver, and in any given case, different perceivers may be constrained to perceive an exigence in a different manner. What we now say about the rhetorical exigence, then, is based *directly* on our interpretation of *Paul's* rhetoric and *his* generic constraints, even while acknowledging the likelihood that Paul adequately surmised his audience's predisposition for the purpose of identification and persuasion.

Rhetorical Exigence

On the basis of our reconstruction of Paul's generic constraints, we may safely assert that Paul's perception of the exigence is that his nascent community remained vulnerable to insecurity, instability and a lack of confidence because of continuing afflictions, especially some type of separation. Given this rhetorical exigence, how then does Paul specifically address his audience's predisposition and how does he adapt the consolatory *topoi* to induce his congregation to maintain their stability? Which consolatory *approach* does Paul take? What is the *goal* of his consolation?

Paul's Consolatory Approach
A typical *approach* of the consolatory writers is to request that their recipients find consolation among their *philia* networks.[3] This is problematic for Paul, however, because the *very source* of the congregation's affliction, in Paul's view at least, is the congregation's own familiar network of support (cf. 2:13-16). Moreover, Paul wants to create an "alternative community,"[4] a community independent of its pre-conversion alliances for a sense of power, prestige and security. To clarify this matter, however, a word is needed about the wide range of relationships and the large number of obligations governed by ancient *philia* networks.

Unfortunately, contemporary scholars often limit ancient *philia* alliances to warm relations between two or more friends. *Philia* networks in the Greco-Roman world, however, could cover a variety of relations, including relations between a person and his/her family, or ethnic group or even city.[5] Furthermore, scholarly concentration on the affection of the relations obscures the otherwise clear set of obligations between members of these alliances.[6] Chief among the obligations were: 1) consistency or faithfulness (Seneca, *Ep.*, 9.8.8; 48.2-4; Pliny, *Ep.*, 9.30.1; Chariton, *Chaereas and Callirhoe*, 8.8.12; Cicero, *De Inventione*, 1.47); 2) comfort in times of distress (Chariton, *Chaereas and Callirhoe*, 3.6.8; 4.4.1; 5.2.6; 8.1.6); 3) remembrance (Ovid, *Tristia*, 1.8.11; *Pontiques*, 3.5.37-38; cf. Nagle 1980:41); 4) support of common causes and toils (Plutarch, *De Amic. Mult.*, 96A, D; cf. Chariton, 4.2.14; 7.1.7);[7] and 5) hatred for common enemies (Plutarch, *De Amic. Mult.*, 96A, B).[8]

A preoccupation with warmth also dilutes the political and economic ramifications of some ancient friendship relations (Stowers 1991:108). Yet many of the discussions about friendship in antiquity involved the political fellowship or unity of a community and the proper responses to the needs (financial, emotional, social, etc.) of its members.[9] Friends often depended on powerful patron-friends who could broker or enhance their security (Plutarch, *Moralia*, 814C; cf. Saller 1982:25, 35, 50; 1989).

Thus, Paul chooses to redefine the lines of friendship-loyalty in light of the congregation's recent conversion (1:9). Paul's letter exploits fictive kinship metaphors,[10] the traditional kiss greeting (*philemati*) among *philia* associates (5:26; see Goldfarb 1992:119), an antithetical typology between friends and flatterers (see above, Chapter Two) and other insider/outsider markers[11] to distinguish the congregation from its former *philia* associates.

Moreover, for Paul, it is from within one's new *philia* that one's power, prestige and security are determined. Given a context of conversion, the members of any new cult would naturally feel the anguish of a loss of identity[12] and the loss of former deference-entitlements, as defined by the larger society or a previous cultic association or philosophy (Kloppenborg 1993:277; cf. Perkins 1989:328). They would also likely writhe over the absence of the *only* few friends they thought they had

(2:17ff). Throughout 1 Thessalonians, then, Paul seeks to console his congregation against disintegration and to compensate for their losses by redefining power, prestige and security. Like the community at Qumran (e.g., 1QS 2:16-17; 9:16-18; 1QH 4.13-14), Paul both defines the world with a strong schismogenetic casting, and redefines power, seeing it as the capacity to endure, outlast or stand firm, rather than the ability to wield excessive force.[13] That the congregation waits on the Lord despite their initial afflictions is one indication that they have this type of power (1:10). Their endurance of suffering where it hurts the most, from their own compatriots, is another (2:14).

Prestige is also redefined. Whatever prestige the congregation once had through its former alliances, their honor or recognition now comes from their work within a new *philia* alliance many of whose members look to them as models of exemplary faith (1:8,9). And given the almost proverbial prestige associated with the universal expansion of a political empire or a religion, the congregation's membership in an extensive network beyond Thessalonica was an important symbol of prestige.

Relatedly, their social advancement and security now is independent of the usual forms of limited social mobility and security within the Greco-Roman world, including any attachment to traditionally powerful figures in their society (Theissen 1972:193-94). In fact, as we have seen, they are challenged to adopt a rustic independence (4:9-12; cf. 2:1-12) and to desist trusting the propagandistic slogans of outsiders (5:3). Their security rests in God who works for their maturation and ensures their ultimate unity despite the forces of separation (3:11-13).

Paul's Consolatory Goal

A typical *goal* of consolatory writers is to assuage, or better, to eradicate a person's (or group's) assent to false propositions, for propositions, not the vicissitudes of life, were considered to be the true sources of the grief (Manning 1981:54). All of the parts of the *dispositio* would function cohesively then to persuade the audience to think a certain way toward external circumstances. In the case of *Ad Marciam*, for example, Seneca's two sets of *exempla*—one historical and one drawn from a stock list—are strategically placed into his argument (Manning, 9). Because each historical example emits moderate emotions, and each of the stock examples emits virtually no emotion at all (Manning, 74), the two sets of *exempla* progressively give a vivid and concrete portrait of the very purpose of the two sets of precepts, namely, to move Marcia from moderate grief to *apatheia* (Manning, 10; cf. Atkinson 1985:868). Even before the *exempla* are listed, however, Seneca lauds Marcia herself (1.5) for the sense of control she exhibited upon the death of her father. The various parts of the letter-essay then gradually reveal Marcia's loss of self-control to be a consequence of her recent assent to false propositions. Marcia's continuing grief exposes the false proposition she has about grief, namely, that it is appropriate (or *natural*) to grieve for loved ones (7.1). In part, Seneca concedes to the Peripatetic's view that some grief is expected; yet according to this view, it is *natural* only to grieve *at the first stroke of misfortune*—not for three years, as with Marcia (Manning, 50).[14] For Seneca, Marcia's extended grief is an indication that she has gone beyond nature—that she has a false opinion about what is *natural*.[15] In part, moreover, Seneca also exposes Marcia's false opinions about external circumstances. That Marcia grieves at all means that she failed to expect adversity (cf. 9.1), for the anticipation of ills, according to the Cyrenaic Cynics and some Stoics, insulates one from the emotional impact of life's vicissitudes (Gregg 1975:16-17; Manning, 50-51).

What then are the false propositions which Paul seeks to assuage or eradicate in 1 Thessalonians? As we have noted in Chapter Three of this study, the precepts in 1 Thess 4 and 5 are designed to remove false opinions about prestige and security. Yet, Paul also appears to question modes of false prestige and false security in earlier parts of the letter. The prestige or glory of the missionaries is measured not in terms of cunning rhetoric, as was the case with many an orator and philosopher of the time, but rather in terms of agonistic *endurance*, rustic independence and pedagogical philanthropy (2:1-12). The security one would expect to find in one's conventional alliances is not an option for the congregation, for in Paul's estimation, the countrymen, like Satan, are hinderers (cf. 2:14-16, 18). In a recent essay, moreover, Wayne Meeks has elucidated the backdrop of honor against which interpreters should understand Paul's ruminations about his recent absence from the community (2:19, 20; cf. 3:13). According to Meeks, Paul understands the prestige he will receive not against the background of a conventional arena, as in, for example, the crowded agora, but before a "transcendent community: God and Christ and their holy ones" (Meeks 1990:308-309). As we shall see, the whole letter bespeaks Paul's emphasis on correct thinking about prestige and security. Yet for now, these limited remarks at least provide us with the beginning of a "thick description" (Geertz 1973: 196-97) of the issues Paul addressed in 1 Thessalonians. To show how Paul sequentially exploited and adopted consolatory conventions, however, we must now turn to the letter's *dispositio*.[16]

Rhetorical *Dispositio*

Given the brief charting of the letter's exigence and Paul's perception of the audience's predisposition, it is now possible to reconstruct the letter's *dispositio* to hear how the letter's basic elements would have reinforced Paul's aims (as we have reconstructed them).[17] Our goal, however, is not to follow the rhetors strictly in delineating the *dispositio* of Paul's argument.[18] Rather, we will follow the simplified *dispositio* of the consolatory letters (exordium, consolatory arguments and peroration) into which writers coopted other philosophical, popular and rhetorical traditions to meet the perceived needs of their audiences.[19] What is important then is the dynamic and progressive flow of Paul's argumentation, not rigid formalistic categories. Moreover, from the authorial audience's perspective, the static categories are not as important as are the relentless echoes and amplification of strategies for "anticipating, circumventing and co-opting audience predisposition in the service of persuasion" (C. R. Smith 1992:76). Accordingly, our sequential reading of Paul's argumentation (from exordium to consolatory arguments to peroration) must be read in consonance with the previously noted rhetorical exigence and audience predisposition. For Paul's *dispositio* is specifically designed to move the audience from its present frame of mind to one he deems to be more favorable.

The entire argument of 1 Thessalonians may be divided into a series of five units: two smaller, framing units which open (1:1-5) and close (5:23-28) the letter; and three temporally distinct, yet thematically interrelated larger units (1:6–2:16; 2:17–3:13 and 4:1–5:22). On the one hand then each large unit is distinguished from its successive unit by a shift in *temporal* perspective. So, in 1:6–2:16, Paul lauds his congregation for imitating and exemplifying true virtue and true security in the wake of the missionaries' foundational visit. Shifting from the foundational visit to the more recent past (2:17–3:13), Paul then extols Timothy as a role model for *how* the community should continue its course of true virtue and true security even while "forcibly" separated from one or more members of its new *philia* network. The next temporal shift from the past to the present (and future) explicitly and preceptually affirms (and requests) the Thessalonians' demonstration of true virtue and true security through its practice of *self-consolation*, even in the face of all circumstances (4:1–5:22).

On the other hand, however, all of the large units are interrelated. So, the concluding section (2:13-16) of 1:6–2:16 becomes, in effect, a basic *partitio* (see Quintilian, *Institutio Oratoria*, 4.2.49) for the second large unit (2:17–3:13), in that it prepares the auditors for a recounting of Paul's recent afflictions since his orphanage or forced separation from the Thessalonians (2:17–3:13). And in turn, the concluding section (3:9-13) of 2:17–3:13 becomes a basic *partitio* for the third large unit (4:1–5:22), in that it prepares the auditors to hear a string of precepts about their roles "toward each other and to all" (*eis allēlous kai eis pantas*, 3:12) as they await the parousia.[20]

Yet, while this overview of 1 Thessalonians gives us the sequential flow of Paul's *dispositio* as his auditors would have heard it, we still need a detailed analysis of the letter to see both 1) the delimiting structure and function of the exordium and peroration and 2) the smaller discrete subunits which determine the demarcation and dynamic movement for each of the large amplification units.

THE RHETORICAL ANALYSIS

In our protracted analysis of Paul's rhetoric, we do not seek the excavation of neatly developed or nicely balanced architectonic patterns. In ancient writings, ecphrastic components were prominent, and these features often offered opportunities for the listeners to become engaged in what otherwise would be viewed as a non-compelling, unintriguing and often paratactically boring writing. Ancient writings also "overlapped at the edges" (Lucian, *De Conscribenda Historia*, 55) in order to maintain a writing's synthesis. We may expect, therefore, *variegated* cues or reception instructions immanent within the text. To assist the modern reader, however, we must first illumine some of the compositional cues. Then, we can proceed with an extended analysis of the opening, the three interrelated units and the closing of 1 Thessalonians.[21]

The Compositional Cues

Previously we have noted three fundamentals of Hellenistic rhetoric with which speakers and writers persuaded their audiences, namely, repetitive composition, exemplification and *ethos* construction of the *dramatis personae*. Looking specifically at repetitive composition, we may now note several cues which were a part of the cultural literacy of the Hellenistic world, and how these cues aided in the memorization, internal organization and amplification of an argument.[22] In the Hellenistic world, textual units were often divided or emphasized through such literary techniques as *anastrophe* (a linking or hooking word inserted at the end of a development and taken up at the beginning of the following development; see *Ad Herennium*, 4.32.44; Parunak 1983:531); *antithesis* (or contrast; *Ad Herennium*, 4.15. 21);*isocolon* (a collection of successive clauses virtually balanced in length and structure; *Ad Herennium*, 4.20.27); transitional markers (the postpositive preposition "for" [*gar*]; or the particles

"therefore" [*oun*]; "finally" [*loipon*]; and "concerning" [*peri*]);
amplification devices—*paralipsis* (or *antiphrasis* [Quintilian, 9.2.
47], the feigned resolve to pass over a matter; *Ad Herennium*,
4.27.37) and *epidiorthosis* (a correction or refinement of a
previous statement; *Ad Herennium*, 4.27.37; Quintilian, 9.1.30);
chiasms (repetition of words, syntactical structures or content
parallels in inverted order); inclusios ("the repetition of the
same word or phrase at or near the beginning and ending of
some unit"; see Dewey 1980:31; Muilenburg 1969:9); and ring
composition (an inclusio pattern "defined by content as opposed to verbal repetition"; Dewey, 32-34; see Moskalew 1982:
122-23).[23]

Other cues also assisted auditors in anticipating or summarizing the basic issues of an argument. An exordium—the beginning part of an argument (Quintilian, 3.8.59; *Rhetoric*, 3.13.
12)—or a *partitio*—a concise section forecasting the content or
themes of the following material (Quintilian, 4.5.22-24)—obviously helped audiences to anticipate subsequent sections of an
argument, while the peroration summarized an entire thesis.[24]
Auditors were also assisted by antithetical typologies, for as we
have seen, antithetical typologies often established basic and
familiar constellation centers into which contrasting *dramatis
personae* could be placed. These compositional cues clear, we
now proceed with a rhetorical analysis of 1 Thessalonians.

The Exordium

Long before chapters 4 and 5, Paul's opening verses (1:1-5)
already begin defining the true virtue and true security which
the missionaries and the congregation share. To be sure, the
opening of Paul's letter appears on the surface to be a rather
simplistic, trite and innocuous set of verses. The opening includes typical epistolary trappings (e.g., a prescript, greetings
and a word of thanks). A terse prescript (1:1a,b) precedes
greetings of grace and peace (1:1c); next there follows a set of
laudations: the first, about the Thessalonians (1:2-4); and the
second, about the missionaries (1:5).

Yet, the sequence of the laudations is telling. Formally, the
sequence mirrors or actually reverses the *order* of the prescript's

senders and receivers, thus establishing the first distinct unit, a thematic chiastic frame (ABB'A') around a central section (C), Paul's greetings (1:1c). Yet, the sequence also forces the reader to compare what the missionaries *know* (*eidotes*, 1:4) about the congregation to what the congregation *knows* (*oidate*, 1:5) about the missionaries. The chiastic pattern thus signals each group's mutual *recognition* of the other's similar and distinctive past.

To see the nature of the singular *ethos* shared between the two groups, however, modern interpreters must join the authorial audience in noting how the opening verses perform the two basic functions of an exordium in the writings of the Hellenistic period (Quintilian, 3.8.59; cf. *Rhetoric*, 3.13.12),[25] namely, 1) to make the hearers well-disposed (Quintilian, 3.8.6; Cicero, *De Inventione*, 1.15.20; cf. *Rhetoric*, 3.14.7);[26] and 2) to foreshadow the keynotes of the argument (Cicero, *De Part. Or.* 27. 97; Quintilian, 3.8.10; cf. *Rhetoric*, 3.13.14). Seeing how 1:1-5 achieves these rhetorical ends should also help us begin to discern Paul's deft ability in fashioning his auditors' views, in evoking pleasant and negative associations and in constructing for his audience appropriate opinions about their shared identities and destinies.

Captatio Benevolentiae

An important function of the exordia found in consolatory letters is to win the goodwill of the audience by including laudatory remarks about the *ethos* of the recipients or the author.[27] Carefully crafted with alliteration, successive participial clauses, a series of isocolonic structures, and an antithetical construction, Paul's opening verses fulfill that function. Beyond the initial alliterative flair in 1:2, that is, the repetition of initial "p" sounds in *pantote peri panton* ("always for all of you"), three successive participle clauses[28] signal what the missionaries remember and know about the congregation's past (2:2-4). Within the second participial clause, moreover, Paul's isocolonic structuring of the Thessalonians' character (their "work of faith and labor of love and steadfastness of hope," 1:3)[29] condenses the congregation's past *ethos* into laudable and familiar typologies in the

Greco-Roman world. As we have noted, work and toil language was often used to describe hard-working rustics and virtuous wise men (see above, Chapter Two). Steadfastness or constancy, moreover, was a well-known convention of *philia* relations (Cicero, *De Inventione*, 1.47) as well as an illustrative trait of the ideal philosopher.[30] For a group facing continuous affliction, this idealizing panegyric would have had a soothing effect. Indeed, its very repetition would have suggested that Paul's nascent community, far from breaking up (cf. 3:5), already possessed the stability of hard workers, true friends or true sages. Their repeated hardships had not altered their course; they remained steadfast.

Yet, Paul moves beyond what the missionaries *know* about the congregation's past *ethos* to state what the congregation *knows* about the missionaries' past *ethos*. How should the authorial audience understand Paul's description of the missionaries' *ethos*? One cue for the auditors is the antithetical construction in 2:4, for antithetical expressions often signaled contrasting constellation centers into which the *dramatis personae* were scripted. Furthermore, because the initial laudation of the congregation began the silhouette for three typological grids—rustic toil, ideal friendship and sage-like maturity—the auditors would easily complete the grids by contrasting the missionaries' gospel with the mere words of those who were stereotypically set in opposition to virtuous workers, friends, and sages, namely, flatterers, unfaithful companions and false philosophers. That is, the auditors would hear Paul saying that the missionaries, unlike the charlatans or flatterers, were notable not for their words alone,[31] but because they aspired to bring others to "full conviction" (*plērophoria pollē*, 1:5).[32] Naturally the complementing panegyric on the missionaries would have had an endearing effect on the auditors, for, then as now, audiences like to hear the similarities they share with a speaker or writer (cf. Aristotle, *Rhetoric*, 2.13.16). Thus, with rhetorical finesse and the portrayal of both parties as sharing the similar *ethos* of hard workers, friends or sages, Paul's two opening laudations (B' and A') accomplish a major function of the exordium—to capture the goodwill of the audience.

Keynotes of the Argumentation

A second goal of the exordia in consolations is to present the key issues or grounds on which an argument will be based.[33] That is, ancient consolatory exordia had an orienting function. Given the structured repetition of "knowledge" diction (*eidotes*, 1:4; *oidate*, 1:5) in the exordium, the auditors could expect Paul to develop the theme of the *mutual recognition* of virtue. Paul does. Later, the auditors are told that the missionaries *and* others recognize the exemplary faithfulness of the congregation (1:8, 9). Likewise, the congregation knows (remembers and can give witness about) the exceptional character of the missionaries (2:1-12).[34] Indeed, because ancient imitation could often involve the acknowledgment and approval of virtuous activity,[35] even Paul's statement about the congregation's emulation of Jesus and the missionaries (1:6) implicitly suggests again the congregation's recognition of the missionaries' virtue.

The auditors could also expect Paul to amplify the typological contrasts begun in the exordium. With the grids already set, Paul simply had to add more detail. So, with antithetical flourish, 2:1-12 invites the authorial audience to see the true virtue of the missionaries. As opposed to the typical flatterers of that day, namely, urbanites, false friends and false philosophers, the missionaries are true friends, sincere philosophers and hard workers (see above, Chapter Two). Moreover, all of the positive *dramatis personae* work, toil or suffer for the habituation of others. The word of God works (*energeitai*) in the congregation (2:13) and with Timothy, God's "co-worker" (*synergon*, 3:2), God works to establish (3:13; cf. 3:2) or enhance the growth and maturity of the congregation. Because both Jesus and the churches of Judea suffer (1:6; 2:14), they too are models worthy of emulation by others who seek maturation. The anonymous "toilers" (*kopiōntas*) in 5:12f. also have the worthy distinction of helping others to come to maturity irrespective of the present and individual levels of their habituation.

On the other hand, all of the negative *dramatis personae* are sculpted as hinderers of the toil and production of the good characters. So, Satan is a blocking character. Again and again, Satan stands in the way of Paul's trip to the congregation

(3:18), a trip ultimately designed to supply whatever may be lacking in the young congregation's faith (3:10). Satan is also a tempter, fully capable of destroying the missionaries' toil (or labor of production) altogether (3:5).

The countrymen of the Judean churches and of the Gentile congregation at Thessalonica are also blockers (cf. 2:14ff). The Judean countrymen stand in the way of the salvation of Gentiles (2:16), and by inference, the Gentile countrymen stand in the way of the maturation of the young congregation at Thessalonica. Even the anonymous "outsiders" (*tous exō*) are capable of hindering the congregation if the congregation depends on the outsiders' resources or takes their advice. For maximum habituation then the congregation is told to develop a rustic independence from outsiders (4:9-12) and they are challenged not to acknowledge the false peace and security propagandized by those outside of their new *philia* network.[36] Instead, *they themselves* must comfort one another and build each other up just as they were doing (5:11; cf. 4:18).[37]

Throughout the letter then Paul develops the antithetical typologies into a "web of ethos." The web holds all of the typologies together and it aids the auditors, from the exordium on, in distinguishing the unique nature of their *philia* alliance.

Beyond the mutual recognition of virtue and the typological contrasts, however, the exordium also signals another theme, the congregation's possession of grace (*charis*) and peace (*eirēnē*). Although the chiastic structure (ABB'A') around the central unit (C) gives special attention to the expressions "grace and peace"(1:1c), the two terms unfortunately have often been interpreted simply as liturgical expressions, without accounting for the political connotation of the currency, nor for the specific situation of the congregation.

In a defiant and paradoxical fashion, however, Paul signals here the congregation's possession of benefits which on the surface could appear to be elusive, especially as the benefits were understood in the patronage exchange of the Greco-Roman world. In the ancient world, grace was a typical expression for favor or beneficence (Hewitt 1927:145). And as Jouette Bassler has noted, "The fundamental meaning of peace in the

Greek tradition is precisely this notion of a state of rest following war, strife, or tribulation (*thlipsis*)" (Bassler 1991:77). This
kind of peace then is what Augustus brought to the Roman
government by quelling its civil wars. Yet, Paul's early acknowledgment of peace to the congregation is marked with paradoxical defiance. Now that the congregation was no longer attached
to its former *philia* and sources of beneficence, how could Paul
speak of grace or beneficence without his words sounding emp-
ty and glib? Now that the community was separated from its
former social networks, with which it would have sustained its
sense of peace, would not Paul's declaration of peace sound
vacuous?

Perhaps so, if that were all that Paul stated. But on either
side of the central unit (1:1c), Paul links the congregation with
their new patron, God the Father (1:1b; 1:2).[38] And because
ancient patrons were viewed as fathers capable of protecting
their clients (D'Angelo 1992), the auditors would understand the
context in which grace and peace were extended. Later, moreover, the authorial audience would hear more about the protec-
tive nature of God, the father-patron. As patron-father, God is
faithful (5:24) and fully capable of assuring the habituation and
protection of all persons within the believers' fictive family
network (3:11-13; 5:23). As patron-father of the congregation
(1:1, 3), the missionaries (3:11, 13; 5:5) and Jesus (1:10), God
deserves constant thanks (1:2; 2:14; 3:9; 5:18) for the maturation of the believers. Within that patronage context then, Paul
can speak defiantly about grace and peace. These benefits are
not elusive and Paul's speech in the exordium is not glib rhetoric. Rather, Paul begins in the exordium to redefine the congregation's sense of belonging. No longer must it look to its former
philia alliances for its identity. Rather, it must rely on the protec-
tive nurturing and stabilizing ability of God, even if on the
surface things go awry.

Whatever else remains to be considered about the exordium's themes must await our investigation of the amplificatory
units which follow the opening. Before turning to the subsequent units however, one final word must be noted about consolatory exordia.

A number of consolations mention the exigence of death almost immediately (*Ad Marciam*, 1.2; *Ad Uxorem*, 608B; *Ad Apollonium*, 102A). Yet, the absence of a word about death in Paul's exordium is not an argument against the consolatory letter as a generic model for 1 Thessalonians, for Paul's argument does not focus on the single distress of death. The separation of Paul (2:17ff), likely an abrupt one, is also a part of the exigence. The *very letter itself*, then, would signal a key distress, the absence of friends from the community. And if Seneca's consolation to his mother (*Ad Helviam*) is considered as an example, Seneca does not mention the exile or separation in his exordium (Book 1); instead, he waits until he has demonstrated Helvia's veteran status in enduring other miseries before referring to the exile as a type of misery (2.5). Paul's approach is similar in that he uses the exordium and the first large amplification unit to demonstrate the veteran status of the Thessalonians before telling his auditors explicitly about his "orphanage" (2:17; cf. *Ad Herennium*, 1.8). Furthermore, for Paul, there may be more potential distresses which he compactly labels as "afflictions." So, Paul does not mention either death or separation initially; instead, he carefully seeks to redefine all distresses within an apocalyptic schema, for he perceives all misfortunes as the typical distresses of all believers who await the parousia.[39]

Thus, an artfully structured opening defines the limits of the letter's initial unit; highlights the goodwill and mutual virtues of the positive *dramatis personae*; and announces the very bases on which Paul's argument will develop. Altogether, moreover, the letter's initial unit (1:1-5) may be outlined as follows:

A 1:1a Epistolary Senders (the missionaries: Paul, Timothy and Silvanus)
B 1:1b Epistolary Receivers (the church of the Thessalonians)
C 1:1c Greetings of Grace and Peace
B' 1:2-4 Recognition of the Congregation's Virtuous Past
A' 1:5 Recognition of the Missionaries' Virtuous Past

The Consolatory Arguments

The three large units (1:6–2:16; 2:17–3:13; 4:1–5:22) roughly correspond to the laudation, examples and precepts sections of some ancient consolations. Each large unit, moreover, is skillfully crafted to inculcate correct thinking about afflictions. The first unit lauds the congregation for its virtuous responses toward afflictions in the past; the second establishes Timothy as a model for aiding others in their habituation despite the recent affliction of separation. The third defines the basic precepts which the congregation has learned and should recall as they continue to model virtuous responses to all changing circumstances.

Consolatory Laudation (1:6–2:16)
Ancient writers often consoled their auditors by *typecasting* them as mature, sage-like figures who have already shown their fortitude in previous struggles. The past success then becomes a basis for dealing with any present or continuing affliction. Accordingly, Plutarch (*Consolatio ad Uxorem*, 608F–610C) praises his wife for her past behavior and encourages her to continue in that way. Seneca (*Ad Helviam*, 2.1–2.4) lauds his mother's veteran status before ever mentioning the present plight (his exile).

A possible problem for Paul in exploiting this same approach is that the Thessalonian congregation was a recently formed community and there does not appear to have been much time between the formation of the church at Thessalonica and Paul's composition of his letter. Yet, Paul also chooses to *typecast* the Thessalonians as mature figures and he does so by detailing distinct moments of their steadfastness. So, in 1:6, Paul highlights the congregation's ability to withstand affliction at the very beginning of the missionaries' work in Thessalonica (1:6). And while the initial suffering marks them as imitators of Paul and the Lord (1:6), another moment of suffering links them with the churches of Judea (2:14). In truth, both mimetic periods occurred at the missionaries' foundational visit, but the *depicted* separation of the moments, along with the protracted self-description of the missionaries in 2:1-12, gives the *appearance* that some time has transpired between the first and the second mimetic moments. The two separate acts of endurance then establish the maturity of the Thessalonians and identify them with the missionaries whose own maturity is measured by a similar marking of *repeated* acts of endurance (2:1-2).[40] On the basis of the congregation's veteran fortitude, moreover, Paul can conclude that his church should be able to face present affliction, whether the affliction is tantamount to his prolonged absence (cf. 2:17ff) or even the potential death of loved ones (cf. 4:13ff). To clarify Paul's laudation, further, however, we must join the authorial audience in hearing the individual and collective force of the discrete subunits of 1:6–2:16.

In 1:6–2:16, the first large unit, two similar short subunits laud the Thessalonians' mimetic behavior (1:6-10 and 2:13-16) and surround a more extended subunit about the missionaries' virtuous acts and motivations (2:1-12). Each short subunit virtually begins with direct remarks about the Thessalonians' imitation[41] and extraordinary reception of the missionaries' word (1:6; 2:13) and ends with an emphasis on God's wrath (1:10; 2:16). And each also includes a digression which clarifies the reception in an indirect way (Lyons 1985:203). So, although Paul begins 1:6-10 with a panegyric about the Thessalonians' joy in affliction (1:6), the elaboration of the panegyric shifts to an account about other believers' recognition of the Thessalonians' virtue (1:7-10).[42] And while 2:13-16 likewise begins with an encomium on the Thessalonians' acceptance of the missionaries' words (2:13),[43] Paul proceeds to amplify that point with another digression, namely, an oblique, but polemical allusion to Gentile opposition (2:14-16). Even with the shift, however, 2:13-16 still highlights the congregation's ideal reception, for implicit in the verses is a contrast between those who are increasing in their maturation as believers of the word of God (2:13) and those who are ever increasing in their role as hinderers of salvation.[44]

Both 1:6-10 and 2:13-16 then are virtually parallel in their general content and form. Heard together, moreover, the two subunits have two functions. In part, they relativize the congregation's losses by showing that they have not suffered alone. Others just as noble have suffered, including persons associated with the founding of believing communities (1:6; 2:15) elsewhere. In part, however, the two subunits also clarify the *ethos* of Paul's congregation. Both speak of the faithfulness of the congregation, either as a *model* of forbearance for others or in their ongoing emulation of other models of forbearance.

Placed in between 1:6-10 and 2:13-16, 2:1-12 evinces the persuasive character of the missionaries' teachings, teachings which secured the "worthy walk" (2:12) of the congregation toward maturation. Connected to 1:6-10 by the hook word (*anastrophe*; see Dewey, 32) "entrance" (*eisodos*) and by the transitional marker "for" (*gar*), 2:1-12 evolves into a series of four sections (2:1-2; 2:3-4; 2:5-8; 2:9-12), each also connected by the preposition "for" (*gar*), and each enhancing the missionaries' *ethos* with laudable remarks about their *continuing* boldness, work of habituation and noble motives. In the first section (2:1-2), with a picture of the missionaries as athletes engaged in much "struggle" (*agōni*, 2:2), Paul highlights the missionaries' boldness in preaching to the Thessalonians, despite the inhospitality received in Philippi. Not only is the boldness consistent, as one would expect for true philosophers, but the athletic imagery is a stock form exploited by the Cynic movement and the Stoic philosophers to depict the truly wise man's struggle (*agōn*; see Epictetus, 3.22.57; 4.10.10; Pfitzner 1967) against his own desires and passions. The antithetical style of the initial section, moreover, sets up a basic contrast which Paul will amplify in the subsequent sections of 2:1-12, namely, a contrast between the missionaries and the typical vain (*kenē*) speakers of that era. 1 Thessalonians 2:1-12 then is not a defense for Paul, nor does the text give the interpreter a mirror image of what any opponents are saying about him, for the antithetical style of speaking was typical among philosophers (cf. Malherbe 1970:217). Rather, 2:3-4, 5-8, 9-12—all variations of a theme—reveal Paul's noble and sincere motivations in contrast to the typical self-serving sophists of his day.[45]

The first (2:3-4) of these subsequent sections, richly textured in antitheses, forces the auditors to distinguish the missionaries from flattering charlatans by showing that the missionaries' aim is to please God rather than persons.[46] Continuing the contrast between the missionaries and sham philosophers, a second section (2:5-8) casts the missionaries as ideal philosophers—

noted for their pedagogical gentleness (2:7);[47] paradigmatic care and self-sufficiency, but not interested in ephemeral glory (2:6).[48] Yet, Paul does not dismiss social prestige altogether; rather, in the final section (2:9-12), he looks ahead to God's kingdom and to the glory of God to which the congregation is called to share (2:12).[49] The missionaries are thus like ideal sages because of their endurance and their proper motivations as true sages, God's emissaries of habituation and as models for others.

Because flatterers were contrasted both to true philosophers and to true friends, however, the missionaries' self-description in 2:1-12 also reiterates the earlier friendship emphasis noted in the exordium (1:1-5). That is, in 2:1-12, Paul's web of *ethos* highlights the mutual *philia* between the missionaries and their young congregation by demonstrating the steadfast beneficent character of the apostles toward their new friends. Abounding in pedagogical imagery, 2:1-12 illustrates the missionaries' faithful assistance in helping the congregation to grow and mature into God's worthy models (2:12). From the congregation's infancy and beyond, the missionaries toiled and worked for the congregation's maturation,[50] even though by right they could have made demands on the congregation (2:6).

Furthermore, because deceitful flatterers were also contrasted to rustics, 2:1-12 also highlights the distinction between the rustic toil and independence of the missionaries and the extravagance and slickness of urban dwellers. Through hard work, the missionaries consistently labored to bring the congregation to maturity, that is, to help them in their eschatological walk toward the kingdom of God into which they were called.

In between the two surrounding subunits about the congregation's *ethos*, then, 2:1-12 is essentially a digressionary panegyric about the missionaries. Yet, because the character of a person or group was often reflected in his/her friends (Saller 1982:109), 2:1-12 implicitly is another portrait of the congregation's *ethos*. The implicit challenge of the portrait moreover is that the congregation, like the missionaries, must continue their role as models for the habituation of others (cf. 1:7ff), despite any difficulties they encounter.

Altogether, the three subunits form a ring composition with the following pattern:

A: Laudation of the Thessalonians' mimetic endurance (1:6-10)
B: The Missionaries' perseverance and noble intentions (2:1-12)
A': Laudation of the Thessalonians' mimetic endurance (2:13-16)

The ring pattern thus lauds the Thessalonians for their impressive and exemplary endurance of suffering in the past and implicitly implores them to continue enduring for the sake of others.

Before moving on now to the next two rings, however, one word is in order. The last part of the first ring is actually a *partitio*[51] for the next ring, 2:17–3:13. While 2:13-16 lauds the Thessalonians for their endurance of repeated suffering, it also implicitly characterizes that suffering as the inhospitable treatment of hinderers toward model figures who seek the salvation of others. In the next ring, Paul explicitly notes the inhospitable treatment the missionaries received, namely, separation from the congregation even as they cultivated the Thessalonians' maturation.

Timothy, a Recent Consolatory Example (2:17–3:13)
When giving *exempla*, consolers had a number of options at their disposal. They could list several *exempla* as Seneca does in *Ad Marciam* (cf. *Ad Helviam*, 15-6; *Ad Polybium*, 14-16.3) or hardly any at all as in Plutarch's *Ad Uxorem* and several of Cicero's letters (*Ad Fam.*, 5.16; 6.3; *Ad Brutum*, 1.9; see Manning 1981:35). Consolers could also list present or past, historical or legendary figures, or any combination, as long as the *exempla* were familiar enough for the readers to discern why the particular paradigms were chosen (see above, Chapter Two). In 2:17–3:13, Paul extols one key figure, Timothy, as a model for the community. Of course, Timothy was known by the community, but to see exactly why he was chosen as a model requires a close reading of the subunits within this second large unit.

In 2:17–3:13, a central subunit (3:1-8) about Timothy's visit to the Thessalonians and his return trip to Paul[52] is placed between two more parallel subunits (2:17-20; 3:9-13) about Paul's aborted and potential trips to the Thessalonians. In the first subunit (2:17-20), an initial statement about aborted trips to the Thessalonians (2:17-18) breaks into a celebration of joy at the expected parousia of Jesus (2:19-20). The expected parousia becomes in effect a context for celebration because at the parousia, separated friends are reunited. And more than that, the parousia becomes the interpretive prism through which Paul can assess present circumstances. Paul's expectation that he will receive a crown for his labors of bringing others to maturity means in effect that he fully expects the community to remain intact (2:20).[53] Thus, the parousia relativizes absence and brings security.

Paul's celebration eventually continues (3:9-13) but only after two flashbacks (3:1-5; 3:6-8) give clarity about other *bases* for his celebration. The first flashback (3:1-5), couched in a small inclusio form, describes Timothy's visit to the Thessalonians. That is, both 3:1-3a and 3:5 essentially highlight Timothy's mission and goal—to console the Thessalonians in the midst of the tempter's afflictions, while a central section, 3:3b-4, contextualizes the afflictions as the presently known and even previously acknowledged lot of all believers. The middle section thus eases the sting of the afflictions, as in the consolatory tradition, by showing how the afflictions were already known (Cicero, *Tusculan Disputations*, 3.23.55), and altogether, the inclusio intimates the nature of *true* failure, namely, the break-up of the community (cf. 2:1). That Timothy was sent to militate against this possibility is indeed a basis for Paul's joy.

A second flashback, Timothy's return to Paul and Silvanus (3:6-8), furnishes another basis for Paul's celebration of joy, the faithfulness of the congregation's goodwill, as given in Timothy's idealized report. Is the report an indication of the congregation's ideal friendship? Or does the report highlight once again the congregation's sage-like steadfastness? Probably both typologies are signaled, for according to Epicurus (*Vita*, 118), a wise man repeatedly speaks well "of his friends, alike when they are present and when they are absent." At any rate, the good news (*euangelisamenou*) Timothy brings (3:6) becomes a source of consolation (*pareklēthēmen*) for Paul as he faces his own hardships (3:7). So, the letter abounds with the theme of mutuality and commonality, here as in the exordium and in the previous large ring composition.

Beginning with 3:9, Paul quickly returns to his celebration of joy, but now his mirth is couched in the sonorous overtones of thanksgiving and prayer (9-13).[54] The entire subunit, 3:9-13, resounds, in form and content, with 2:17-20. Both subunits include rhetorical questions (2:19; 3:9); both speak of Paul's desire to see the Thessalonians face to face (2:17; 3:10); and both include double references to Paul's "joy" (chara).[55]

Both 2:17-20 and 3:9-13 also draw on the familiar Greco-Roman imagery of the parousia of an official or ruler (2:19a; 3:13) to challenge the Thessalonians about their interpretive prism for understanding circumstances. Familiar to all persons at that time, a parousia event was the arrival of an important official and his entourage (Deissmann 1910:372; cf. Bruce 1982:57). In Paul's dramatization, Jesus' parousia is a glorious apocalyptic affair at which Paul and all of the saints will accompany Jesus. However distressful the separation and regardless of the hindrances plotted by Satan, the parousia event assures the believers that they will see each other again.

Yet, there is one basic difference between the two parallel subunits (2:17-20 and 3:9-13), for the latter subunit is a *partitio*. That is, 3:9-13 speaks of the missionaries' assurance that God, the patron-father, will bring the congregation to full maturity in their love for each other and for all; and indeed, all of 4:1–5:22 bespeaks the mature (or holy and distinctive living) to which the Thessalonians are called as they await the parousia.[56] In 4:1–5:22, Paul will highlight the community's continuous growth and maturation (4:1, 10), including the various ways in which members of the community may help each other (4:18; 5:11; cf. 5:12-15). The next large unit will also amplify the ways in which the community may love outsiders, that is, by presenting themselves as a "good form" (euschēmonōs, 4:12) for the unbelievers. Yet as a *partitio*, these upcoming matters are now simply set forth in 3:9-13 without elaboration;[57] at present, some matters then must remain opaque.

Formally then the auditors of the letter would have understood 2:17–3:13 as a ring composition patterned as follows:

A: Aborted trips to Paul's congregation
. . . coming of the Lord (2:17-20)
B: Timothy's visit to the Thessalonians
and his subsequent return to Paul and Silvanus (3:1-8)
A': Expected trip to Paul's congregation
. . . coming of the Lord (3:9-13)

Given the central position of 3:1-8, along with its own internal structure of "travel" flashbacks, the auditors are forced to pay careful attention to Timothy's scripted role as he travels to the congregation and to Paul. Yet, how would the authorial audience understand Timothy's role and why is the description of his work so necessary in-between the first and third subunits? In 3:1-8, he is extolled as a model for his work of habituation. Drawn as God's co-worker (*synergon*, 3:2), he performs a role similar to God's role. That is, both work to bring others to stability or maturity (cf. 3:2, 13). Yet, Timothy's work in 3:1-8 mimics the virtuous work of the missionaries in 2:1-12. In the earlier passage, the missionaries brought the gospel (2:4, 9) and offered exhortation and comfort (2:11) for the young church's habituation. Timothy likewise performs these roles: he brings the gospel (3:2, 6); and he comforts both the congregation and Paul (3:2, 7). The noticeable difference between 2:1-12 and 3:1-8, however, is that in the latter case, a separation has occurred.

Timothy's critical function then is to model the act of habituation when members of the *philia* are *separated* from each other. Yet, the congregation has indeed aided the habituation of others even when it was separated from them, for the congregation's faith was known as a model of maturity in Macedonia and Achaea (1:7, 8). For the first time, however, the auditors are nudged to see how "comfort" must be included in their practices of habituation. Repeatedly, Timothy "comforts" (3:2, 7), as indeed did the missionaries collectively at the foundational visit (2:1-12). In the next unit then Paul will press the congregation to *comfort one another* (4:13; 5:11) with the practices they already know and are using (4:1, 9). Moreover, the congregation *must* console each other during their moments of affliction because in so doing they provide a virtuous model of true security for others, both for the believers elsewhere (like the missionaries) and for the outsiders.

Consolatory Precepts (4:1–5:22)

In the consolatory tradition, precepts established the fundamentals which helped or could help the *dramatis personae* react properly to the vagaries of life.[58] The precepts were designed to help habituate the auditor(s) in a type of teaching leading *to maturity or to the maintenance of maturity* in any and all circumstances. Functioning in a way similar to the consolatory precepts then is the *last* large unit in Paul's earliest extant letter, 4:1–5:22.[59]

Before elucidating the discrete subunits of the last large unit, however, we would do well to note again that Paul's auditors would be constrained to make connections between this unit and the preceding materials. Obviously, as we have seen, the *partitio* character of 3:9-13 forces the authorial audience to make connections. Yet, the exploitation of consolatory diction (4:1, 10, 18; 5:11, 14), as well as the repeated emphasis on walking (*peripatein*, 4:1 [twice]; 2:12), should suggest to the auditors that there is also a connection between the last large unit and the subunit 2:1-12, where the missionaries' self-description dramatizes rustic toil, ideal friendship and sage-like wisdom. In 4:1–5:22, then, Paul will press the congregation to honor ideal friendship and true wisdom by *adhering to* the same precepts given to them at the foundational visit (4:1, 2, 6, 9, 11). Moreover, just as the missionaries' honor came through hard work rather than self-aggrandizement (2:1-12), so must the congregation gain its honor through its hard work for the habituation of others (cf. 4:9-12; 5:12-15).

Formally speaking, in 4:1–5:22, a middle subunit of thematically similar apocalyptic material (4:13–5:11), is placed in the middle of two parallel subunits (4:1-12; 5:12-22),[60] each of which provides a true knowledge about proper relations with others.

Both 4:1-12 and 5:12-22 are subunits designed to help the congregation in its consistent walk by habituating the congregation against faulty judgments. Obviously, both subunits emphasize consistency, an ideal of true friendship and true wisdom.[61] The former does so with acknowledgments of the congregation's present adherence to the teachings of the apostles (4:1) and of

God (4:10); and the latter, with calls for sustained joy, prayer and thanksgiving, in all circumstances (4:16-18). Both subunits also emphasize the habituation of the congregation, and yet, because many earlier interpreters failed to appropriate the background of habituation conventions accessible to Paul's audience, it is necessary to read these precepts against the grain of traditional interpretations.[62]

In the habituation currency of that day persons received progress in their moral development through reasonings about what was a true judgment as opposed to a false one, because, in fact, the truth could free individuals to react properly in all situations (Stowers 1988:277). Accordingly, in 4:1-8, Paul's introductory acknowledgment of the Thessalonians' knowledge of how to walk (worthy of God, cf. 2:12) and please God (4:1-2) is followed by 1) a gnomic truth about sanctification as the will of God (4:3); 2) three injunctions, which essentially contrast the holy life to a false judgment about life (4:4-6a); and 3) three bases for shunning the false judgments (4:6b-8).

Unfortunately, much energy has been spent on the identification of the problems of the injunctions (see Yarbrough 1984: 66). What has escaped notice, however, is that God is portrayed as an avenger for all of the injunctions.[63] The faulty judgment which lies at the heart of each of the acts condemned is the inability to see beyond one's present acts, the failure to understand that God is an avenger of any impieties toward others. The vices then are miniature portraits exemplifying faulty judgments about relations with others. They also depict actions which, because they are similar to the wantonness of the "countrymen's" behavior (2:13-16), are likely viewed as acts which hinder habituation.[64]

In 4:9-12, Paul does not switch to a new theme.[65] Rather, Paul employs *paralipsis* and *epidiorthosis* (L. *correctio*), two well-known rhetorical devices, to sharpen his discussion of "walking" (4:12),[66] that is, to clarify more specifically how the community can exhibit virtuous behavior. Indeed, Paul's epithet for the congregation—"taught by God" (4:9)—as well as his insistence that the community practice living consistently, quietly and self-sufficiently are yet other ways of demonstrating how the community can love "one another" (*allēlous*, 4:9) and others as well (cf. 3:12). Paul acknowledges that there is nothing more to say about the congregation's love for other believers, except that the church should love more and more (4:10) in discrete acts. In so doing, moreover, the congregation will provide a "good form" (*euschēmonōs*) for the outsiders (4:12).[67]

Paul's specific points in 4:9-12, couched as they are in the currency of philosophical polemic, are not given then as a warning that Paul wants to distinguish the church from Epicurean or Cynic groups in Thessalonica.[68] Likewise, Paul neither chastises his own congregation for not working[69] nor makes a specific indictment against a philosophical group. As we have noted, even rhetoric based on an actual group need not indicate the truth about that group (see above, Chapter Two). The polemic in 4:9-12 calls attention, however, to an earlier *ethos* construction in which Paul demonstrated the missionaries' rustic independence and noble motives as they led others in an "walk" toward God's kingdom (2:12). The challenge now is for the community to do the same, to act as a moral model (a "good form") of rustic independence and "walking" before the outsiders. Thus, the polemic in 4:9-12 is best understood when we recall that hard work and toil were frequently noted by ancient consolers to indicate the tests or trials which identified persons chosen by God to be an example of endurance for others.[70] Within the rhetorical development of Paul's letter, moreover, Paul uses the work metaphors to indicate a social prestige based on endurance. Thus, Paul puts the admonitions of 4:9-12 before his congregation to demonstrate a type of social prestige which the congregation has apart from their former *philia* networks. But what is the "good form" which Paul commends to his auditors? We will return to this matter later.

Because 5:12-22 follows a middle subunit about the congregation's reactions to external circumstances, Paul essentially amplifies 5:11, with reminders about the need for mutual care, individuated habituation and even a concern for outsiders (5:12-15).[71] As with 4:1-12, then, Paul demonstrates how the community can habituate each other rather than hinder each other. In order to treat the issue of false and true judgments once again, moreover, Paul concludes the subunit with a sonorous set of staccato stacked maxims (5:16-22). The form signals that Paul will soon draw the letter to a close, but the point of the maxims is constancy,[72] the very ideal of true friendship and true wisdom previously attributed to both the missionaries and the congregation. The point is that true concern for others is constant, despite changing circumstances. Paul seems even to account for circumstances which the community has not already experienced, for his gnomic sayings emphasize the community's own careful moral reasoning about the "good" in any given circumstance. Once *they* have determined the good or what the Greco-Roman culture understood as the fitting and appropriate thing to do in a given situation, they must hold onto it (5: 21).[73]

Yet, how would Paul's auditors understand 4:13–5:11? We have already observed that the ending of the subunit, namely, 5:11, is related to 5:12-22. Is there a connection between 4:1-12 and 4:13–5:11? Most assuredly! Given Paul's previous remarks about providing a "good form" (*euschēmonōs*, 4:12), Paul now idealizes the "good form" in terms of the believers' responses to difficulties. That is, because wise persons in the ancient world were often identified through their struggles or difficulties (cf. Newman 1988:150), the next section, 4:13–5:11, dramatizes how the believers may exemplify a model form for outsiders. Believers must demonstrate a difference in their perspectives or their understandings about changing circumstances. Death is not a problem for the believers because their security lies in a cosmic union (at the parousia) which overcomes death (4:15-17). The sudden coming of God's wrath is not a problem both because believers know that present forms of peace and security are fleeting (5:3ff) and because, again, believers will ultimately be with God and will escape God's wrath (5:9-10). All that they need now do is to remain as vigilant as soldiers.[74] Moreover, in the final expressions of both 4:13-18 and 5:1-11, Paul enjoins his congregation to *comfort one another* (4:18, *Hōste parakaleite allēlous*; 5:11 *Dio parakaleite allēlous*) because of the eschatological guarantees.

Before concluding the analysis of this section, however, a few words are in order about the situation of the audience presupposed in 4:13–5:11, for the verses have been the source of much controversy.[75] Because the basic drive of the precepts is to give illustrative examples of how the community may exhibit "good form," it is highly unlikely that Paul *at any point* is chastising his congregation about misconstruing what he said about the death of others or the day of the Lord. Rather, Paul clarifies here what he could only briefly mention in the *partitio* of the previous large unit. Here he amplifies what it means to love others outside of the fellowship. Essentially, the community demonstrates love outside of the fellowship by showing, in its responses to changing circumstances, what are the true judgments about the circumstances beyond their control.

The first changing circumstance forwarded as an illustration is death. Had some members of the congregation already died? Several scholars seem to think so (e.g., Lüdemann 1984:237-38; Grundy 1987:167). These scholars contend that the grief of the Thessalonians had arisen because they did not expect their members to die before the parousia. This kind of interpretation is not entirely defenseless. If members of the congregation had died, others remaining could well have wondered whether or not the parousia could overcome mortal separation. Paul then could have assured those remaining that the death and resurrection of Jesus is the basis upon which they can hope for the resurrection of their dead loved ones and that according to the word of the Lord, *all* of the members of the church at Thessalonica would be together again (4:14-18).

Another alternative interpretation, however, is to interpret 4:13-18 as Paul's effort to sketch contrasting views about death for the sake of exemplifying the believers' "good form." To join the authorial audience in properly understanding the contrast, however, we must recall Cicero's ruminations about consolatory precepts, including the precepts which deal with an untimely death or "with a life spent without obtaining office and fame" (*Tusculan Disputations*, 3.81). Plutarch is perhaps even more helpful, however, because he elaborates the popular sentiments about those who die untimely deaths (*Ad Apollonium*, 113C; cf. *Ad Uxorem*, 611C):

> some may assert that there need not be mourning for every death, but only for untimely death, because of the failure of the dead to gain what are commonly held to be the advantages of life, such as marriage, education, manhood, citizenship, or public office.

In 4:13-18, Paul likely draws on the consolatory *topos* of grief for the *fameless* victim in order to distinguish his *philia* network from others. For Paul who has previously associated hope (*elpis*) with *prestige* at the parousia (2:19), the congregation has no need to grieve as others who have no *hope* (*elpida*, 4:13) *for the eschatological prestige of those who die untimely*, precisely because the event of the parousia accomodates for the loss of possible prestige on earth. Rather than suffer a disadvantage, the dead in Christ—now or at any time—would actually gain the benefit of being the *first* to join Jesus in a glorious parousia. Furthermore, Paul rather craftily reinforces his point about the advantage of the dead in Christ by using the expression "shall be snatched up" (*harpagēsometha*, 4:17), the very Greco-Roman coinage associated with "untimely deaths."[76] Yet Paul exploits the coinage not to describe what will happen to the dead in Christ, but rather to illumine what will happen to those remaining.

Moreover, the event of the parousia brings *permanent* prestige and true security for the congregation. That is, Paul is not saying that those who have fallen asleep will momentarily be "with Jesus" (*syn auto*, 4:14) at the parousia; or that the remaining ones, including himself, will simply for a while be "with them" (*syn autois*, 4:17a)—Jesus and the sleeping ones. Instead, the force of Paul's repeated use of the preposition *syn* ("with") is to signal the congregation's permanent union; it will *always* be "with the Lord" (*syn kyrio*, 4:17b). Thus, in the first illustration of "good form," the congregation can show their model character by remaining hopeful whenever the external circumstance of death comes untimely. Ultimately, the permanence of the "Lord's" order and all the prestige attending it compensate for an untimely death and become the basis both for the community's internal comfort and its external model for outsiders.

As with 4:13-18, moreover, there is no need to read 5:1-11 as the congregation's misunderstanding of Paul's teachings about the day of the Lord. Rather, in a paraliptical way,[77] Paul again uses *epidiorthosis* to get to the heart of an issue, and in this case, the issue is a set of assumptions about God's wrath. In Greco-Roman culture, the wrath of a god was often associated with death.[78] Mindful that outsiders may have understood death as a sign of God's wrath, Paul distinguishes his congregation from others in terms of what believers think about God's wrath. To be sure, the wrath of God is something over which no one has control. Yet, for the congregation, they are secure and they have the hope of salvation, not destruction (5:9). Thus, Paul has not really shifted his discussion. He continues to distinguish his alternative community from others by demonstrating the proper responses they should have over things that are not in their sphere of control. Moreover, social prestige is still an issue in 5:1-11. True (eschatological) prestige, however, is not found in ephemeral internal peace and external security (5:3);[79] rather, it is found in *permanent* salvation. Indeed, Paul's repetition of *syn* ("with") yet a fourth time (5:10) clearly conveys to the authorial audience the *permanence* of their prestige, that is the *permanence* of being in the presence of their benefactor.

Altogether then, the Consolatory Precepts section may be outlined as follows:

A   4:1-12   Proper Judgments about Relations with Others
B   4:13–5:11   Proper Judgments about Circumstances Beyond the Congregation's Control
A' 5:12-22   Proper Judgments about Relations with Others

Paul's third large ring thus includes precepts necessary for the habituation of Paul's congregation. Essentially the precepts commend the congregation toward an eschatological orientation both in their relations to others and in their reactions to circumstances beyond their control. Of course, these precepts have already been modeled in the previous large units, both in the early friendly behavior of the missionaries and the congregation and in the recent exemplary character of Timothy. Here in the third ring, Paul simply wants the congregation to continue doing what it has already been doing, to continue acting as members of an alternative community of friends by strengthening one another. Only now Paul *explicitly* says that a part of their practice of habituation must include comforting one another. In so doing, the congregation maintains its role as a virtuous model for others.

Peroration

The last part of Paul's letter (5:23-28) is a distinctive unit carefully scripted to achieve the basic functions of a peroration, that is, to excite the emotions of the audience while summarizing or amplifying the argument's theses.[80] In his outline of the letter's disposition, Kennedy (1984:142) suggests that the peroration is found only in 5:23-24[81] and that verses 25-28 form a closure. I would include verses 25-28 in the peroration itself, however, for the following reasons.[82] First, if the additional verses are included, then, the entire peroration would include a nicely balanced structure: two intercessory prayers (5:23-24; 5:28) surrounding three final commands (5:25-27). Second, in line with the affective function of a peroration, the philophronetic terms (e.g., brother, greet, kiss) in those final commands would heighten the peroration's emotional charge (25-28). Third, in line with the amplificatory function of a peroration, all of 5:23-28 aids in summarizing the letter's argument. The repetition of the word "brothers" [*Adelphoi* (5:25), *adelphous* (5:26), *adelphois* (5:27)] signals, once again, the mutual recognition which sets the Thessalonians apart from others. And the references to "holiness" (*hagiasai*, 5:23; *hagiō*, 5:26) or to a sense of being "called" (*kalōn*, 5:24) remind the Thessalonians of their distinctiveness as a community as they await the parousia.

In the exordium, Paul began his letter with a generous word of praise about the congregation and the missionaries. In the peroration, he ends his letter with an impressive and sweeping encomium about God and Jesus. In a form richly textured in prayer, Paul closes his letter with reminders of the community's ultimate source of stability and security (5:23-28).[83] Only the God of peace can bring full sanctification (or full maturation) to the Thessalonians (5:23); God alone can keep them and render them blameless (fully matured) at the parousia (5:23).[84] Indeed, according to Paul, the faithful, beneficent God will do it (5:24); and the congregation will have the grace or beneficence of Jesus with them (5:28).

CONCLUSION

From the apostle Paul to Toni Morrison, the fate of a writer's work is left in the hands of succeeding interpreters. Recently, with the rise of rhetorical studies of 1 Thessalonians, however, the fate of Paul's earliest extant letter has changed. This chapter, standing as a witness to that change, has revealed the exquisite skill of Paul in constructing his audience. Exploiting some of the fundamentals of Hellenistic rhetoric (repetitive composition, exemplification and *ethos* construction), along with the *topoi* and form of the ancient consolatory letter, Paul sequentially constructs an audience of veteran sufferers whose exemplary faith is a model for others. Having already participated in the habituation of others, the congregation is now admonished to continue that practice, especially through words and acts of comfort to one another. And having already responded to previous afflictions in a virtuous manner, the congregation is asked to respond to the recent distress, separation, in the same manner.

Given Paul's construction of his audience and the exigence of his letter, how then can we approach the sparse extratextual material and gain an understanding of the shape and contours of Paul's congregation? What are the misgivings about previous studies which have assayed to relate the letter to the environs of Thessalonica? To answer these questions, we now turn to the final chapter.

5

THE
AUDIENCE
AND
EXTRA-TEXTUAL
EVIDENCE

Thirty years ago, in the blistering heat of an August day, in the shadow of the Lincoln Memorial, and in the midst of a crowd of more than 250,000 persons, Martin Luther King, Jr., delivered a speech that immortalized him as a dreamer, a visionary, a prophet peering down through the telescope of time to find an era unsoiled by oppression and unsullied by discrimination. Yet King's famous "I Have a Dream" speech was not a rash of utopian rhetoric unconnected to the local and national environments of the local and national television audiences which heard him speak.[1] King's "financial metaphors" resonated with many of the marchers' banners and placards which critiqued the United States for its defaulting economic promises to black people. And his "covenant metaphor" resonated both with the country's (Judeo-Christian) perception of itself as a chosen and covenanted people and with the political covenant theory reflected in the long tradition of American self-critique and reform.[2] In using these two metaphors then, King was able to relate his challenge to a nation using vernaculars *germane* to the actual environments or contexts in which his audiences moved, lived, thought and worked.

In 1 Thessalonians, Paul also used diction which reflected the environments of his authorial audience at Thessalonica.

Having thoroughly investigated the letter of consolation as a generic model for 1 Thessalonians, we must now determine the *relevant* cultural evidence which might help us better to understand both Paul's rhetoric and his audience's environments. The benefit of the previous chapters in this regard is that we safeguard ourselves against *misreading* symbolic cues for social and political realities. That is, with a knowledge of the letter's stereotypical rhetoric, particularly in depicting its basic antithetical typologies (friends *vs.* flatterers; urbanites *vs.* rustics; and the true sage vs. the false one), we are able to access the cultural situation of the Thessalonians without facilely relating Paul's rhetoric to irrelevant extra-textual evidence about the Thessalonians. Accordingly, in this chapter, we shall show that the ideology of beneficence, a complex related to ancient notions of friendship, rustic toil and virtuous wisdom (cf. pp. 56, 63, 64), was particularly pervasive in Thessalonica. Moreover, we will show that Paul likely used the language of beneficence because that diction would add persuasion to his argument about the social prestige of the Thessalonians.

WORK, SOCIAL STANDING AND METAPHOR

Before looking at the ancient benefaction complex, however, we turn first to assess scholarly discussions about the rhetoric of "work" in 1 Thessalonians and the social standing of the Thessalonians.[3] This discussion is important because it helps us to understand the extreme caution scholars must take in moving from a writer's rhetoric to reality.

On the social status of the church at Thessalonica, Robert Jewett avers that the church was made up of lower class artisans experiencing relative deprivation (1986:121). In this instance, he goes against the claims of Acts 17 (a chapter which pictures the Thessalonians as well-to-do) and notes instead the presumable poverty level of all the Macedonians as drawn by Paul in 2 Cor 8:2-4. Also, he alludes to the self-sufficient references in 1 Thess 2:9-12 and 2 Thess 3:6 to suggest that Paul's audience was made up mostly of employees or of self-employed laborers (120). Furthermore, he accepts Wayne Meeks' contention that the "typical" Pauline Christian in the Pauline churches was "a free artisan or small trader" (121; cf. Meeks 1983:73). The most salient problem with this assessment of social status is that it is one-dimensional. In his *First Urban Christians*, Meeks issues the caveat that the term "lower class" is not appropriate "because it ignores the multi-dimensionality of stratification prevalent in the Greek city" (1983:54). In this sense, therefore, an artisan did not have to be poor or uneducated.[4] Another problem with Jewett's assessment is that it infers from the terms of self-sufficiency that all of the Thessalonians were drawn from the same stock, i.e., that all of the Thessalonians were artisans. Finally, even 2 Cor 8:2-4 has to be used cautiously and should be respected as a piece of rhetoric. As Meeks notes, the abysmal poverty of the Macedonians in 2 Corinthians "may partly be hyperbole occasioned by the structure of Paul's rhetoric in 2 Corinthians 8 which depends upon the antithesis of 'poverty' and 'wealth,' 'abundance' and 'lack,' leading on to the goal, beloved also by Hellenistic moralists, of 'equity' (*isotēs*, v. 14)" (66). In 1 Thessalonians as we have seen, however, "work" terms are related to the similarities in *ethos* (moral character) between the apostles and their congregation at Thessalonica. Beyond this claim, however, the text is silent on any notion of a homogeneous professional background for the members of the church.

Abraham Malherbe (1987) begins his discussion of the Thessalonians' social status with remarks about the social location of Paul. Malherbe avers that a private workshop within an *insula* house (a Greco-Roman urban apartment building with accommodations for both living quarters and shops) was the most appropriate setting for relatively mobile persons like Paul and his associates (7-18). At odds with this contention, of course, are the claim of Acts 17 that the setting of Paul's preaching in Thessalonica was the synagogue and the claim of some modern interpreters that the most appropriate setting for Paul as a philosopher was the marketplace. Malherbe critiques Luke's portrait by noting Luke's theologically motivated pattern of letting Paul first go to the synagogue and then to the nonproselyte Gentile (in order to show that the center of God's activity in the world had changed from Jerusalem to Rome). Likewise,

Malherbe endeavors to adjust the thinking of modern interpreters on the issue of Paul's social location by noting that Paul's style of discourse reflects a more private setting as opposed to a public one. Then, Malherbe, in looking directly at the social location of the Thessalonians, notes "Luke's tendency to mention socially prominent and economically well-off converts" (16-17) and resolves to side with 2 Cor 8 in Paul's depiction of the Macedonians as extremely poor.

Malherbe's thesis, while commendable in many ways, also has problems. Given the state of archaeological research on Thessalonica today, the murky waters of social location and social standing cannot be fully cleared until there is a systematic excavation of Thessalonica and a full-blown subsequent study.[5] At present, however, many arguments remain tenuous and are often vitiated by the available evidence. For example, even though Malherbe wants to limit Paul's preaching to the private workshop as opposed to the public agora (marketplace), excavations at Thessalonica have unearthed an agora which "occupied two insulae."[6]

Also, although Malherbe wants to limit the social status of the *insula* house dwellers to manual laborers and tradespeople, there is evidence to indicate a variety of *insula* houses occupied by persons from a variety of social standings.[7] Furthermore, as we have noted before, Paul's admonitions toward "work" must be set within the rhetoric of 1 Thessalonians to understand the role the admonitions play in Paul's argument just as the "extreme poverty" of the Macedonians needs to be set within the rhetoric of 2 Cor 8. In the case of 1 Thessalonians, Paul's "work" metaphor describes the effort of persons (including God) who seek to provide for and protect the new *philia* as a compensation for certain losses and tensions sustained in the congregation's turn from its former alliances.

THE ANCIENT BENEFACTION COMPLEX

Holland Hendrix (1984; 1986; 1991) has well illumined the importance of benefaction at Thessalonica, so that we need only adumbrate the complex of beneficence along with a brief history of Thessalonica's long acquaintance with beneficence ideology before demonstrating Paul's exploitation of the ideology to identify with his audience.

The Greco-Roman ideology of patronage was a system of mediated social relations intended both to support the legally designated status distinctions between the elite and the inferiors and to channel power to those regions without direct and proximate access to the chief governing authorities. Given the system's inherent reciprocity ethic, the monarchical authorities could expect praise, obedience and faithfulness in return for their benefactions; and likewise, a variety of mediating brokers (e.g., prefects, procurators, client-kings, high level soldiers and special assistants) could expect deference, particularly when they secured favors for the inhabitants of their provinces.[8]

Moreover, the ancient symbiotic system of beneficence actually affected every aspect of Greek and Roman society— "the ways in which people view their world, earn their living, associate with their fellow treasurers, and relate to the state administration" (Saller 1982:3). Thus, in relations among most individuals, the beneficence system of exchange not only governed a variety of household relations (most notably that between master and slave and freedperson; D. Martin 1990:25), but it extended as well to other personal relations: some between unequal free persons who masked their superior-inferior relations with the euphemistic diction of friendship; and others between social peers who exchanged personal favors for themselves or for their own individual clients (Saller, 138). And in interstate and international relations, a person or ethnic group or even a whole nation could grant cultural and administrative favors to empires, provinces and municipalities (Rogers 1991:93).

Naturally, the most notable example of this form of beneficence is that of the emperors. For while interstate and international beneficence had long since been a part of the Romans' cultural and political ideology, with the rise of Augustus and the emergence of an era of peace, a long expected new age was initiated (Koester 1992:11-13); Augustus was cherished as the greatest universal benefactor; and his dynastic successors were legitimated as the supreme rulers of the oikoumenē.

Whatever its forms, however, the ideology of exchange was inherently linked to social prestige for the patron and the client. Those able to provide benefactions gained "prominence and social powers" (Meeks 1983:12) and those receiving the benefits either protected and enhanced their honor through the offer of gratitude (L. *gratia*) and loyalty or they elicited stern rebuke and public disfavor when these expected reciprocities were withheld.[9]

THESSALONICA AND BENEFICENCE

From its founding under the Greeks to its annexation by the Romans, the inhabitants of Thessalonica had long understood the symbiotic system of beneficence.[10] In the pattern of Alexander and his father, Philip, one of Alexander's generals, Cassander, both founded the city of Thessalonica and became its benefactor in 316 BCE; and Rome, which saw itself as the patron of colonies soon received this role when Thessalonica was annexed in 146 BCE (see Meeks 1983:11-12; Jewett 1986: 123).

Even beyond 146 BCE, however, beneficence played a role in shaping the Thessalonians' political ideology, for the city was granted the status of a "free city" (Jewett, 123) in 42 BCE for its cooperation with Octavian (Augustus), the victor of the last civil war of the Roman republic. While Rome granted the city the right to hold a citizens' assembly and to mint its own coins, Thessalonica returned the favor with *inscriptional and numismatic* honors—all designed to cultivate "the new ruler's [Augustus'] confidence in the city's loyalty to him and his successors" (Jewett, 337). Faced as it was with burgeoning municipal taxes (Hendrix 1984:283), Thessalonica, like Greek cities elsewhere, also extended deference to a number of local and foreign Romans, both to reciprocate present favors and to insure future ones (Holland, 336; Jewett, 126). So great was the respect that the Greeks had for the Roman network of power, moreover, that many Greeks, as is evidenced by their epitaphs, actively sought Roman citizenship (Meyer 1990:93).

1 THESSALONIANS AND THE BENEFICENCE COMPLEX

Against this background of the beneficence ideology of the ancient world and Thessalonica's participation in it, we may now understand more clearly the peculiar audience situation which Paul *constructed and addressed* in 1 Thessalonians. To do so, however, we must recall the results of the previous chapter and imaginatively re-write a history of the church at Thessalonica.

Paul's congregation at Thessalonica, a nascent group of gentile believers (1:9; cf. 2:13-16), experienced afflictions (1:6; 3:13) of one sort or another. Whether these afflictions were mental or physical or both is difficult to say. Karl Donfried (1985:342-47) and Robert Jewett (1986:39-40) propose that the afflictions were some form of physical persecution. Abraham Malherbe (1987:36-52) relates the afflictions to the mental anguish often associated in ancient times with religious and intellectual dislocation. My own perspective resonates with Malherbe's perspective, but it is not mutually exclusive to the other standard interpretation. I suggest that the affliction is the loss of social prestige associated with the congregation's connections to their former *philia* networks.

In order both to identify with his congregation and to connect his rhetoric to what his congregation faced daily in their environment, Paul saturates his apocalyptic hermeneutic with beneficence currency. Key for Paul in his letter is the exploitation of the same benefactor ideology operative in Thessalonica and elsewhere in Greco-Roman society, but for Paul social prestige is not linked to honor before men. Instead, it entails pleasing God (2:4, 15; 4:1) and sharing in the glory and triumph of God (2:12), a true glory to be fully consummated at the parousia of Jesus (2:20). What Paul has to do in the letter therefore is to exploit the benefactor currency, though he insists that God is the patron, not human beings.

Furthermore, with his schismogenetic rhetoric, Paul separates the community from its former *philia* networks within which the patronage ideology would have been operative. With familiar antithetical typologies, Paul drives a wedge between the congregation and its members' former affiliations. The congregation's true friends, says Paul, are not solely in Thessalonica but in Athens, Judea, other parts of Macedonia, Achaea and even heaven. Like rustics, the congregation can survive tough times independent of outsiders. With the virtuous apostles, moreover, the congregation have a model for their own maturation and habituation. Paul suggests that the community has already survived despite its infancy; it will yet survive. The congregation will make it by working together independently of outsiders (cf. 4:9-12). Ultimately, however, they will survive because God, like an imperial magistrate (5:24), is faithful. God will see them through.

CONCLUSION

While rhetoric is always a construct, it is not unrelated to the real environments of an audience. Martin Luther King, Jr.'s "I Have a Dream" speech resonated with the economic vernacular of the participants in the March on Washington in 1963 and Paul's rhetoric spoke to the local, regional and imperial beneficence ideology of the Thessalonians. Moreover, Paul's exploitation of the beneficence complex worked on two levels. On the one hand, Paul's consolatory writing challenged the merits of the normal networks of power and social mobility. With rustic independence, the community need not depend on its former *philia* alliances, for the prestige of the old alliances, in Paul's estimation, is associated with deception and a false sense of glory. On the other hand, Paul's consolatory writing certainly acknowledges God as a patron. For Paul, God's power is not simply demonstrated in the deity's worship in several regions. It is also shown in God's extension of security to the congregation.

CONCLUSION

Fundamental for this study is the contention that ancient writings are highly strategic and culturally specific. Paul's rhetoric does not simply respond to a situation, but it also constructs one; thus, the discovery of an audience profile must take into consideration ancient strategies of constructing an audience. And as I have argued, the work/toil metaphors do not provide an audience profile of "relatively deprived" individuals because strategically the metaphors aid the audience in viewing itself as veteran sufferers able to handle any new difficulty (even one caused by a separation of an audience from its former *philia* networks).

Thus, any description of Paul's congregation at Thessalonica must begin at least with a circumscription of some of the commonplace literary conventions with which 1 Thessalonians and other first century CE writings were written. Chapter Two's discussion of repetitive composition, exemplification and *ethos* construction did just that. The discussion of these fundamentals of Hellenistic persuasion clearly helped us to avoid the imposition of an anachronistic literary repertoire onto Paul's earliest extant writing, even as the discussion convinced us that the task of describing Paul's congregation is freighted with difficulty. Accordingly, we discovered that even a presumably opaque description such as "work with your own hands" (1 Thess 4:11) must not quickly be read as an indication of the congregation's "artisan" vocation. Instead, this particular "work" diction has to be interpreted carefully within the repetitive set of "work" metaphors found throughout the letter. Fortunately, Paul's exploitation of specific genre, the consolatory letter, gives contemporary interpreters additional help in defining the contours of Paul's community, for genres, when understood as more than formal features, reflect specific social contexts and social interaction.

Our discovery in Chapter Three was that Paul wrote the letter to help his friends at Thessalonica overcome one or more major misfortunes. Through an apocalyptic interpretive scheme, along with the rich philosophical and popular *topoi* of ancient consolation, Paul penned a work the aim of which was to help the community know how it could survive within its new *philia* network. But how did Paul sequentially develop his argument?

Chapter Four, a protracted rhetorical analysis, furnished the details of Paul's carefully developed argument. In addition, we were able to see that the key distress, at least read through our reconstruction of Paul's interpretive constraints, was the separation of the apostle from his congregation and that any other distress (e.g., death), whether actually occurring or not, was simply illustrative to Paul's argument. Chapter Four also aided in solidifying our earlier conclusion that the "work" metaphor in 1 Thessalonians was not an indication of a specific social profile; rather, it was a strategic part of Paul's stereotypical construction of the community as independent, wise rustics.

Chapter Five then suggested that if the relationship between Paul's rhetorical image of the congregation and their actual (political and social) circumstances can be seen at all, the most fruitful course would be to examine the beneficence ideology of the community. Paul's exploitation of beneficence ideology pictures God as a patron in ways in which the community could have drawn on its prior understandings of patronage in Thessalonica's local and wider spheres of power. With God as their father-patron, the community could feel protected and could expect to have "true" peace within and "true" security from without, even when things went awry.

Thus, reconstructing the profile of an ancient audience is a meticulous chore, not merely because language is not transparent, a critical insight offered by many a postmodernist,[1] but also because the critic must recover the sparse notices on the ancient means of persuading audiences, especially those notices on the creation of idealistic images as compensation for a particular audience's momentary plights. Interpretations which overlook these means or strategies thus miss hearing some of the hidden and explicit appeals of ancient texts—a knowledge of which, I think, is necessary for ascertaining an audience profile.

Two final sets of remarks are necessary about this study. First, a word is in order about changing ideologies. In the first chapter of this monograph, I noted that an interpretation written to a modernist or postmodernist audience is hardly finished until one has critiqued the plusses and minuses of an ancient text's ideological framework in light of the current sensibilities shaped by the geopolitical shifts and changing intellectual paradigms of the intervening centuries. On the surface, 1 Thessalonians has much to commend it for application to our times—the creation of an alternative community which resists paltry forms of security, the reinforcement of hermeneutical frameworks and vital supportive networks for those who face suffering, the construction of power as stability under pressure and not as the ability to wield force. Problematic for our times, however, is the patriarchal nature of the genre which Paul employs, for the consolatory genre, for all of its benefits, construes stability and maturity in androcentric terms. The consolatory tradition viewed "weakness" (*asthenēs* in *Ad Apollonium*, 113A; *infirmitate* in *Ad Marciam*, 1.1); grieving (*Ad Helviam*, 3.2; *Ad Polybium*, 6.1-2); and lack of self-control (*Ad Helviam*, 14.2) as the *natural* attributes of women. Moreover, within this tradition, men were idealized, and when the tradition praised a female, as in the case of Marcia (*Ad Marciam*, 16.1), the praise was given precisely because the woman was regarded as different from the Greco-Roman conventional portrait of women, that is, for possessing the qualities which were defined in that society to be the *natural prerogative solely of males.*[2]

Notwithstanding the momentary "pedagogical nurse" imagery in 1 Thessalonians (2:7),[3] or Paul's generally acknowledged acceptance of women vis-à-vis the writers of later works in the Deutero-Pauline school, Paul fundamentally construes maturation in 1 Thessalonians, in accordance with the consolatory tradition, in the accepted patriarchal symbols of the period. God is conceived as one with a kingdom (2:12) and father language is exploited to speak both about the missionaries (and the church, by extension) and God. Thus, the Thessalonians' relationships to God and the missionaries are largely drawn in male imagery. As the exordium (1:1, 3) intimates, and the rest of the letter confirms, God is both father of the Thessalonians and Paul (along with his companions, 3:11, 13; 5:5) and of Jesus (1:10). And as we have seen, the attribution of the father-hood of God is, in part, a way of consoling the Thessalonians by reminding them of their roles as models of endurance. The family connections are not only expressed through repeated references to God as father, but also through references to the believing community as "brothers" and as "sons."[4] The appella-tion "brother" in the exordium (1:4) and beyond (2:1, 9, 14, 17; 3:2, 7; 4:1, 9, 10, 13; 5:1, 4, 12, 14, 25, 26, 27) is not an inno-cuous attribute, nor it is merely transitional;[5] rather, it lin-guistically represents the predominant and distinctive capacity of the believing community—they are "brothers" in suffering.[6] Re-latedly, the inverse of God's fatherhood is the believer's sonship, and for Paul, that sonship is a guarantee that the be-liever is destined for salvation rather than ultimate destruction (5:9). The familial repertoire therefore affirms God's selection of the missionaries and the Thessalonians as models, and not as victims of divine retribution. It also creates a fictive kinship into which the congregation may now see itself apart from its past *philia* relations. Furthermore, in light of the community's long familiarity with beneficence ideology, Paul likely exploited the patriarchal language to compensate the community for its losses sustains in its recent detachment from former networks of power.[7]

At the same time, however, the patriarchal language of 1 Thessalonians forced the ancient female members of the authorial audience to become "male" if they wished to join the ranks of the authorial audience. Indeed, they are forced to accept the implicit, patriarchal point of view of the genre. That is, as they are exhorted to shun "weakness" and instability, the very emotions which this popular genre defined as "effeminate," they are asked, in fact, to act "manly."

And for all contemporary readers who join the ranks of the authorial audience of 1 Thessalonians, the generic constraints and diction ask us to accept the construction of God as a king (cf. 2:12) and a father, thus reifying and legitimating a patriarchal view of the world by sacralizing it. Of course, some, quite naively, will try to dismiss the issue by saying that Paul lived at a different time. Others, more astutely may argue that Paul—even with his rhetorical skills—could not possibly have invested his rhetoric with the kind of hegemonic codes often detected by some contemporary ideological critics.[8] Yet, the point is that the text, whenever it was written and for whatever purposes, still has influence today.[9] That is, successive generations, viewing Paul's writings as paradigmatic and therefore authoritative, have been influenced by the patriarchy of the letter.[10] The father-children pastoral ethic, especially inherent in the contemporary hierarchical modality of ordination, is yet alive today (Tolbert 1990:8); and this pastoral ethic gains support in part from those canonical texts which construe leadership predominantly with patriarchal imagery.[11] What is needed then is an "ethically responsible" critique[12] against the abstraction of "transcendent truths" from Paul's contingent and historically conditioned writings, particularly when those "truths" perpetuate the dominance of one group over another. What is needed, moreover, is a challenge to the dominant reading conventions of *any* age,[13] especially those readings which force all readers, including women, to become like males (to become "fathers") in order to identify with the (patriarchal) points of view of the texts (Tolbert 1990:17, 18).

Second, perhaps the book's occasional interest in Paul as an author or in the social situation of the letter will prove disturbing to many trained in poststructuralist thought, for the writings of Roland Barthes (e.g., 1977) and Michel Foucault (e.g., 1977), to name a couple of early poststructuralists, decry talk about "authors" and any other pre-existing referents of a text. The incentive behind my interests in this work, however, has not been to write a final, definitive statement on 1 Thessalonians as if discussions about a biographical author or of ancient consolation could guarantee a single, privileged and authoritative interpretation of 1 Thessalonians.[14] To the contrary, what the study offers is a plausible interpretation which, because it is rooted in a reconstruction of the social, political and economic circumstances of an urban Pauline community, offers the contemporary critic (within one or more interpretive communities espousing the merits and validity of public debate)[15] the advantage of critiquing the ancient popular reading conventions of consolation for their contributions to patriarchy in Paul and in the continuing Western world.

Far from being a definitive statement, what I write is only a first chapter in continuing interpretations about people who have known intense suffering. Others will cast a light in dark corners which I have not seen, thus making this work a better one than I alone could possibly make it. My only hope is that, perhaps because of *continuing* interpretations of suffering, we may creatively find some timely and consoling words for the wretched of the earth among us—in Bosnia (not far from ancient Thessalonica), in Haiti and Rwanda and right here in the United States, especially in our inner cities. If so, this book and its challenges will have made a difference.

NOTES

BIBLIOGRAPHY

INDEXES

NOTES

NOTES TO INTRODUCTION

[1] The term "authorial audience" was coined by Peter Rabinowitz (1977:126). My investigation of Paul's authorial audience does not rely on 2 Thessalonians, and there are two reasons for its omission. First, there is still no current consensus on the authenticity of 2 Thessalonians. Even Robert Jewett (1986:17), who uses 1 and 2 Thessalonians in his argument, can only assert that 2 Thessalonians is "probably Pauline"; and if one were to concede to Jewett's argument, a number of interlocking inferences would have to be accepted to give credence to his claims.

Second, 1 Thessalonians is not an insufficient datum for the determination of Paul's view of the audience. While both letters may provide more frames in the cinematic sketch of the audience, 1 Thessalonians is not without its own frames, and if they are focused clearly and closely, they can show us an outline of the audience with some definition and proportion. For more on my objections to using 2 Thessalonians as a basis for constructing Paul's authorial audience, see my dissertation (1989:21-23).

NOTES TO CHAPTER ONE: CHARTING A COURSE FOR INTERPRETATION

[1] Contemporary interpreters of letters traditionally attributed to Paul continue a dispute begun in the 18th century and solidified in the 19th and 20th centuries, namely, the dispute over the letters' authorship. To help distinguish this problem from that of a letter's integral character, scholars have used the terms "authenticity" and "integrity," the former term referring to the question, "Did Paul write a work?," and the later term to the question, "Is the canonical work a complete and single literary composition or does it have a composite character?" Whereas thirteen letters in the New Testament canon purport to be from Paul, there is general agreement that only seven (Romans, 1 Corinthians, 2 Corinthians, Galatians, Philippians, 1 Thessalonians, and Philemon) are indisputably authentic Pauline letters. The remaining six letters (Ephesians, Colossians, 2 Thessalonians, and the Pastoral epistles [1 and 2 Timothy and Titus]) are deemed to be inauthentic, and of the six, the Pastorals are the most disputed, with scholars favoring the Pauline authorship of Colossians and 2 Thessalonians

(particularly, the latter) more so than Ephesians. For more on these matters, see Keck and Furnish 1984:16-17.

[2] For an excellent discussion of the Tübingen school's influence on the interpretation of 1 Thessalonians, see Jewett (1986:4-5); he provides (1-60) a detailed history of scholarship on the most widely discussed issues in contemporary study of 1 and 2 Thessalonians.

[3] The heterogeneity of literature refers to all of the various formal (genre, stylistic level, characterization, etc.) and extratextual elements (e.g., historically conditioned socio-political valuations) on which an interpreter might focus (see further, Alter 1989:214-217). Also, see Paul B. Armstrong who suggests that a text needs to be considered as "a field of different possible meanings, each correlated to a particular method of interpretation" (1990:22).

[4] In ancient writing, the oblique and the unstated added intrigue and challenged the reader/listener to participate in reconstructing the author's/speaker's rhetorical moves. For a discussion on this rhetorical feature, known as *significatio* (Quintilian, 8.3.83), see the epilogue in Woodman and Powell (1992:213-214).

[5] On common sense as a cultural practice or "cultural artifact," see Meeks 1983:5.

[6] On the pervasive character of the current anti-objectivist epistemology in anthropology, history, hermeneutics, the sciences and literature, see Fish 1989:344-45.

[7] I do not worry that others may find a different set of validating criteria, now or at a later point in history. The particular elements in the set are not as crucial as that individual members of an interpretive community can agree on a set. Thus, the fundamental principle is that the criteria can find public agreement in some interpretive community. A new set may emerge tomorrow, for by then some of the philosophical presuppositions about language, literature and communication will have changed. On the possibility of different test sets, see Armstrong 1990:ix. On interpretive communities, see Fish 1980.

[8] The "Western introspective conscience" foisted on Pauline scholarship of Romans 7, for example, presents a view of Paul which belongs much more to the 16th century piety of Luther than to Paul whose concern here was the relationship between Jews and Gentiles.

[9] On Eastern Christianity's reading of Romans 7 and on the "introspective conscience" as a Western phenomenon begun by Augustine and continued by Luther, see Stendahl 1976:82-85.

[10] Among the mine field of theoretical positions in literary criticism, I take a moderate, pragmatist position, that is, I understand meaning to be developed through an interaction between the text and the reader, and for this position, I am largely indebted to the critical discussions of audiences in the works of Hans Jauss (1982:18-19), Wolfgang Iser (1974) and Peter Rabinowitz (1987).

[11] Both Jewett and Malherbe also mention 2 Thess 3:6 as evi-

dence of the Thessalonians' social location, though Malherbe does not make the claim that Paul authored both letters.

[12] On differing conceptions of the rhetorical situation, see Bitzer 1968:1-14; Vatz 1973:154-61. In a sterling critique of Lloyd Bitzer's conception of the "rhetorical situation," Richard Vatz argues that Bitzer naively thinks that a speaker's rhetoric simply responds to a rhetorical situation. Vatz (155) asserts that Bitzer evidently assumes that meaning "emanates, so to speak, from the thing [described], and as such there is no process involved in its formation." For Vatz, however, a speaker's "choice of events to communicate" (156) and his/her "linguistic depiction" (157) create or construct the rhetorical situation.

[13] That is not to say, however, that we cannot learn general information from Acts based on the shared literary conventions which centuries of ancient people shared with each other.

NOTES TO CHAPTER TWO:
RECONSTRUCTING HELLENISTIC RHETORIC

[1] Of course, it is impossible in the final analysis to interpret a text without the influences of one's own cultural biases and presuppositions. As Tony Woodman and Jonathan Powell note: "No scholar can claim a superhuman objectivity. We cannot remain uninfluenced by the fashions and preoccupations of our own time, but we can at least try to be aware of our own limitations and to allow for the subjective elements in our judgments" (1992:210-211).

[2] Railton 1991:11.

[3] The classicist Lane Cooper noted that Lincoln's fondness for birth images is actually an extension of the "metaphor of the dedication of a child;" thus, the movement of the text is from "conceiving" to "bringing forth" to "dedicating" (1966:243).

[4] As with Mary Ann Tolbert (1989:37 n.5), I speak about the Hellenistic period in a cultural sense, not a mere political sense. Thus, for the purposes of this study, the Hellenistic period extends roughly from the 4th century BCE, with the rise of Alexander the Great, to the 4th century CE, at the "triumph of Christianity." Moreover, by using the term "Hellenistic," I am not suggesting that the Greeks fostered a unilateral acculturation of people within the Mediterranean basin. Obviously, all of the cultures of that period mixed and obviously the term "Hellenistic" is a construct to indicate one, though certainly not the only, great influence on that historical period.

[5] Even Lincoln's vernacular rhythms and taut speech must be viewed as cultural constructs expected and appreciated by the auditors of an age shifting from a slower agrarian culture to a faster technological one. On the relationship between Lincoln's style and the cultural shifts of the 19th century, see Wills 1992:174. On the shifts themselves, see Gilmore 1985:1-4.

[6] Again, we cannot totally avoid reading texts through our own cultural lenses, but without apprising ourselves of the cultural repertoire of the ancient world, we give easy access to our own theological constructs.

[7] On fate in the ancient world, David Tiede suggests that: "The catalog of treatises in Hellenistic philosophy includes numerous titles concerned with fate, fortune, providence [and] chance" (1980:3).

[8] As we shall soon see, *philia* networks could include members of one's family, friends and even one's whole race. However constituted, the fundamental requirement is a system of shared obligations, interests and even enemies. See the rhetorical analysis section in chapter four for more details.

[9] Alexander's expansionist policies became a paradigm for his successors, whether Greek or Roman. The expansion of an empire was viewed as a sign of power. In Roman imperial times, for example, Augustus and other emperors (Claudius, Trajan, Septimius Severus) sought to extend their boundaries to gain prestige for themselves and for Rome. On Alexander's policies as a pattern, see Romm 1992:121-123, 137. Also, see Virgil, *Aeneid*, 6.785-88. On the Roman imperial expansion, see Ramage 1987; Nicolet 1991:15; Campbell 1984:138, 141.

[10] According to Wayne Meeks, 1 Thessalonians extends "the lines of friendship to other groups of Christians elsewhere in Macedonia, in Achaia, and in Judea" (1983:114). Note also that Paul says that the faith of the Thessalonians was known "everywhere" (1:8). The hyperbole tacitly confirms the prestige of the Thessalonians and the power of Paul's religion.

[11] The *paideia* included a number of authors (poets like Homer and Hesiod; tragedians like Sophocles and Aeschylus; and historians like Herodotus and Thucydides) from whose works literary styles and moral lessons were taught. See Riesenberg 1992:50.

[12] As Burton Mack suggests, "The agora, the gymnasium, and the theatre, as well as the family courtyard and the city chambers, were all good places to give and hear an interesting speech" (1990: 31). And as George Kennedy has noted: "the rhetorical theory of the schools found its immediate application in almost every form of oral and written communication; in official documents and public letters, in private correspondence, in law courts and assemblies, in speeches at festivals and commemorations, and in literary composition in both prose and verse" (1984:10).

[13] While the scanty remnants of Greco-Roman culture suggests that *epistolography* was only scarcely treated in the progymnasmata (the elementary exercises used in Greek and Roman schools), rhetoric certainly had an influence on letter-writing. Letter-writing, rhetorical analysis and rhetorical elaboration were all a part of the grammar school curriculum, even before a student advanced on to a more comprehensive study of rhetoric in the Rhetorical School. Thus, anyone

who had been taught to write a letter would also have been trained in some of the fundamentals of rhetoric. (On letter-writing in the grammar school curriculum, see J. White 1986:189; Kennedy 1969:47). Moreover, see Quintilian, who (in his portrait of an ideal curriculum) allowed for overlap between some grammarians and rhetoricians as long as the former realize "that they are teaching rhetoric when they do so" (1.1.6). We should note also that although Demetrius (*Elocution*, 223) suggests that letters should be free of rhetorical elaboration, after Demetrius, "a good deal of art found its way into the letter, with the sanction of the rhetors" (Fiore 1986:43 n. 69). In fact, the art of rhetoric found its way into Greco-Roman letters because letter-writers coopted specific epistolary genres which themselves were influenced by the rhetors.

[14] The question of whether Paul knew rhetorical theory need not concern us. As Joachim Classen suggests, "anyone who could write Greek as effectively as Saint Paul did must have read a good deal of works written in Greek, thus imbibing applied rhetoric from others, even if he never heard of any rules of rhetorical theory; so even if one could prove that Saint Paul was not familiar with the rhetorical theory of the Greeks, it can hardly be denied that he knew it in its applied form" (1992:323).

[15] Under the influence of rhetoric, historians like Herodotus and Thucydides artistically reconstructed events of the recent past. Under the same influence, subsequent writers of histories, biographies and panegyrics recast the formative and historical factors of powerful figures in accordance with aspects of the hero's *ethos* deemed worthy of imitation. On the earlier writers, see Badian 1992:190. On the later writers, see Koester 1982:134.

[16] Ancient rhetors differed on the exact number of categories necessary for the *dispositio* or rhetorical design of an argument. As Paul Douglas Hahn (1990:54-55) has noted, a number of rhetors following Isocrates and Aristotle, changed their basic four-part design (*proomium, diegēsis, pisteis, epilogos* in Isocrates; *proomium, prothesis, pisteis, epilogos* in Aristotle) to either a five-fold design (cf. Cicero and Quintilian) or a 6-fold design (cf. Cicero and the author of the *Ad Herennium*). That Cicero could use either a five-fold or six-fold division shows, moreover, that the rhetorical design structures were not fixed. See Kirby 1990:116.

[17] The conventions chosen were selected because they convincingly demonstrate how rhetoric functioned on the level of image and symbol as I discussed in the previous chapter.

[18] The rhetorical handbooks, as programmatic distillations of actual practice, largely treated the effects of rhetoric on the ear. On the rhetors' interest in the effects of language on the ear, see Aida Spencer (1984), particularly her discussion on Aristotle, Demetrius and Longinus. Cf. Cicero, *De Oratore*, 50.168.

[19] On amplification (*expolitio*), see *Ad Herennium*, 4.42.54-56; Cicero, *De Oratore*, 63.212; Dionysius of Halicarnassus, *Demosthenes*, 48.

[20] This kind of steering can easily be seen in Virgil's *Aeneid*, for, as Walter Moskalew has noted, the large repetitive patterns "bring out the parallels or contrasts between the respective scenes. This allows for thematic development and hence for the possibility of altering the reader's perception of a scene or character" (1982:122).

[21] Of course, some texts may well have interpolations, but the caution I raise is against a proclivity toward interpolation theories without due consideration for the role that repetition played in the ancient world.

[22] Not just letters, but all Greco-Roman writings used repetitive forms—Homer's epics, historiography and popular narratives. Even dramas exploited oral compositional features to connect their episodes, choral odes and speeches. As David H. Porter has noted, several "of the extant Greek tragedies display a striking parallelism between their overall movement and the movement of their component parts" (1971:465).

[23] Quintilian, 4.3.14; Cicero, *De Inventione*, 1.51.97; 2.77.311-12; *De Oratore* 2.19.80; 3.53.203.

[24] In the tragedies, for example, the parallelism varied in length, and was occasionally jarred (for some aesthetic effect) by contrapuntal scenes. See Porter 1971:489.

[25] On *synthesis*, see Long., *Sublime*, 40.2; Dion., *On Word Arrangement*, 3. On the motivations of the few ancient writers opposed to *synthesis*, see Freudenburg 1993:132-173.

[26] As we shall see, *loipon* in 4:1 (often translated as "finally"), is a transitional marker indicating the final set of three large, interrelated structures in 1 Thessalonians. On the similar role of *loipon* in Philippians 4:8, see Watson 1988:82. On the transitional character of *peri de* (often translated as "concerning") in 4:1, 9; 5:1, see M. Mitchell 1989a: 229-256. Cf. J. White 1986:211. Also, note that Robert Hodgson avers that in 4:1 "Paul shifts to exhortation whose directness in view of chapters 1-3 catches the reader by surprise" (1986:3-91. Another way of seeing this shift is to note the pervasiveness of the infinitive *ginomai* ("to happen") in the first three chapters, while imperatives are pervasive only in the last two chapters. Thus, we can say with a great deal of certainty that 3:9-13 creates a distinguishable—though not radical—break between the first three chapters and the last two chapters of 1 Thessalonians.

[27] On the maxims in 1 Thess 5:12-22, see Sampley 1991:96. On the staccato arrangement of the maxims, see Roetzel 1972:367-383. Compare the ancient rhetors' discussions on maxims: Aristotle, *Rhetoric*, 2.21; Quintilian, 8.5.3; *Ad Herennium*, 4.17.24.

[28] This description of exemplification, though applied by Richard Whitaker to characterize the mythological paradigms used by elegists, actually is an apt description of all ancient examples. See Whitaker 1983:11.

[29] As Quintilian noted, examples may be complete or partial (4. 11.6), depending on the knowledge of the audience, which, in every case would be more culturally competent than the modern interpreter.

[30] On the untrustworthiness of ancient political and philosophical invective, encomium, and even history, see C. Edwards 1993:10-12.

[31] Exemplification, as a form of an argument's amplification, was taught as a part of the progymnasmata (rhetorical exercises) in the ancient schools of Rhetoric and probably in the curriculum of the ancient grammar schools as well. See Watson 1993:96; Robbins 1988:20.

[32] On Aristotle's perception of the "easy intelligibility" of examples, despite his reticence in using inductive forms of argumentation, see Fiore 1986:28. On Aristotle's reticence and the subsequent increase in the use of examples, even over deductive forms, in the Hellenistic period, see Donelson 1986:100.

[33] "You must go to the scene of action, first, because men put more faith in their eyes than in their ears, and second, because the way is long if one follows precepts, but short and helpful, if one follows patterns [exempla]." Seneca, Ep., 6.3-5 or 6.4 or 6.5.

[34] The author of the third century BCE handbook Rhetorica ad Alexandrum (8.21-23) asserts that "Examples (paradeigmata) are actions that have occurred previously and are similar to, or the opposite of, those which we are now discussing." Later, Cicero focuses primarily on the parallel type both in his youthful work, De Inventione (1.30.49), and his more mature work, Topica (10.41-45). Still later, Quintilian delineates example forms into three types: similar, dissimilar and contrary (5.11.5-16).

[35] For the distinction between historical and invented examples, see Aristotle, Rhetoric, 2.20.2. Later, the writer of Ad Herennium (4.2-4; 4.45.59–48.61) shows a preference for the invented type of example.

[36] So familiar were the mythological examples used in the Augustan love poetry of Tibullus, Ovid and Propertius, that "the bare mention of a particular mythological character or incident would be sufficient to evoke a wide range of associations which the elegists could exploit as they wished for their various purposes." See Whitaker 1983:15.

[37] On the use of vice and virtue lists to "fill in the lineaments of an example," see Fiore 1986:73-75.

[38] In fact, the moralizing element was true even in the literature of the classical period. "The habit of using examples from history and myth to illustrate a moral lesson is very old in classical tradition. It can be found as early as Homer, where the great heroes of the still earlier past are used as models and quoted in speeches, so that their successors can imitate their virtues, avoid their errors" (Highet 1976:67-68).

The moralizing element is also found in the encomiastic and paraenetic literature of Isocrates (Evagoras, Helen, To Nicocles) and Xenophon of Athens (Cyropaedia). In fact, Isocrates himself asserts

(*Evagoras*, 77): "For we exhort young men to the study of philosophy by praising others in order that they, emulating those who are eulogized, may desire to adopt the same pursuits." On Xenophon, see Halliwell 1990:32-59; cf. Stowers 1986:91.

Ancient *exempla* also played the related role of giving authority to a writer's work. In his analysis of Seneca, Thomas Habinik asserts that "His [Seneca's] treaties lay claim to the authority of parental advice, mentor's guidance, natural and familial exempla, and self-interrogation in the presence of intimates—all conventional aristocratic modes of control over thought, word, and action, in Rome as in other traditional societies." See Habinik 1992:189.

[39] See Seneca, *Ep.* 29.4; 52.2, 7; 52.8; 100.12. Cf. Fiore 1986: 89-90. On Seneca's view of himself as a "fellow-patient," see Tietze 1992:55. On Seneca's use of medical examples in his epistles, see Seneca, *Ep.* 22.1; 27.1; 40.5; 50.4; 64.8; 72.5-6; 94.24; 95.29.

[40] For example, in Chariton's *Chaereas and Callirhoe*, Callirhoe is drawn in the image of the beautiful Helen of Troy.

[41] As we shall see, in 1 Thessalonians 2:1-12, Paul repeatedly clarifies the distinctiveness of the missionaries from the typical sham philosophers.

[42] North 1979:137. Homer's *dramatis personae* often speak about their past reputations for persuasive purposes. Note especially, the character Nestor who revels about his previous heroic exploits (145-46). Of course, Homer does not use the term *ethos*, but his works are concerned with the character of the various *dramatis personae*.

[43] The particular parts of the speaker's character which Aristotle noted are the speaker's intelligence, virtue, goodwill. See Aristotle, *Rhetoric*, 2.1.5.

[44] In the west, it is Homer from whose works a list of *aretai* or virtues was initially formulated as the basis for panegyric and invective. See North 1979:137.

[45] See Aristotle, *Rhetoric*, 3.16.11; *Ad Herennium*, 3.8.15; Cicero, *De Inventione*, 1.5.7; cf. 2.52.157ff; Quintilian, *Inst.*, 3.4.6-16.

[46] See Hermogenes, 46-49; Aelius, *Theon*, 3.251. Cf. Vasaly 1993:90-91.

[47] According to Vasaly (1993:89), "the Roman orator was encouraged to consider various aspects of places in making emotional appeals." Cf. Quintilian, 5.10.41; Cicero, *De Legibus*, 2.4. On character denigration or enhancement through association with other characters, see Saller 1982:109.

[48] The neo-Platonist Plutarch often berated other ethnic, religious and philosophical groups, including the Jews (*Moralia*, 169D); the Stoics (*Moralia* 1033B-1057C) and the Epicureans (*Moralia*, 1086C-1107C).

Robert Hall avers that ancient orators "omitted, altered, rearranged, or fabricated events for maximum effect. Even when truthful, they continued their accounts so that events suggested proofs to be advanced later, cut out any events not essential to their argument, and attributed motives to their characters to make plausible their interpretation of events" (1991:313-314).

[49] As Scot McKnight asserts: "Rhetorically potent language is used throughout the ancient world to erect, fortify, and maintain the boundaries that distinguish one religious community from another or to separate, within the same religious community, the obedient from the disobedient" (1993:55).

For a list of polemics used by Jews against other Jews, see Johnson 1989:436-441.

[50] The Epicureans did not deny the existence of gods, but given their mechanistic view of the universe, they argued that "the gods did not involve themselves in this world" (Stowers 1990:277).

[51] On the role of typologies in assisting writers to "draw on the resentments and bitterness, [and the] sympathies and hopes" of an audience, see Vasaly 1985:19.

[52] In his *Pro Roscio*, Cicero contrasts both the rustic and the urbanite and two types of rustics, one young and the other old. See Vasaly 1985:9-11.

[53] We can infer that the community was composed of Gentiles from two clues. First, in 1:9, Paul notes that the Thessalonians "turned to God from idols." The statement would not make sense for a Jewish audience. Second, if 2:13-16 is taken as authentic (and I will say more about this matter later), the original ethnic lines of demarcation are made clear in 2:14. Paul suggests that the Thessalonians are suffering from their countrymen the same things that the churches in Judea suffered from the Jews. The analogy infers that the Thessalonian countrymen were not Jews, and thus, neither were the Thessalonians.

While Acts gives the impression that Paul's converts at Thessalonica were both Jews and Gentiles (Acts 17:4), I have two misgivings about including Luke's accounting of Paul's travels in my consideration of the ethnic constitution of Paul's congregation. For one, with an audience-oriented approach, Acts would not have been a part of the specific literary repertoire of the authorial audience of 1 Thessalonians. Second, Acts has a pattern similar to Chariton's *Chaereas and Callirhoe*. In Chariton, virtually everywhere the two protagonists go, they find a shrine to Aphrodite, the goddess of love, before which they offer their worship. Likewise, in Acts, Paul finds Jews and a Jewish synagogue wherever his travels take him. The significance of the prevalence of the Jews in all places is that the universality of the Jews' god is highlighted if Luke can demonstrate that this god is worshipped all over the Mediterranean.

Given the cosmopolitan character of Thessalonica, one may speculate that there was a synagogue there, as some scholars have done, but to the extent of our archaeological data today, there is *no evidence* for a synagogue in Thessalonica at this early period.

[54] Of course, the type of slander Paul chooses (that of labeling the "outsiders" as ignorant and enslaved by passions) was used by Jews against other Jews and by Gentiles as well. See Josephus, *Antiquities* 1.15.91. Also, cf. Philo, *Cherubim*, 17; 4 Maccabees 1:1, 3; 2:2, 3; Pseudo-Phocylides, 194. Also, compare the Gentile writer Plutarch ("The Education of Children," 7F), who says: "to rule pleasure (*hēdonōn*) by reason marks the wise man, and not every man can master his passion (*orges*)."

[55] There is some question about whether Paul speaks here about *some* Jews "who killed the Lord Jesus" (2:15) or the Jews as a whole. Frank Gilliard (1989) suggests that Paul's regular use of the articular participle is to restrict the meaning of the noun it modifies. Thus, the articular participle "who . . . killed" (*ton . . . apokteinanton*) would have been limited to a particular group of Jews, not all of them. Taking a different perspective, Donald Hagner (1993:133, 134 n. 24) asserts that Paul broadens his scope from the Judean Jews in 2:14 to all the Jews (2:15, 16) "who were unreceptive to the gospel and who opposed Paul's missionary work." While one need not turn to later letters of Paul to settle an issue about an earlier one, "the Jews" opposing Paul's work were certainly not "all the Jews." Moreover, as we shall see, Paul's vituperative rhetoric actually castigated the gentile countrymen whose actions were similar to those attributed to some of the Jews.

[56] Plutarch's *Moralia* (48E-74E) includes an entire discussion on the friendship vs. flatterer typology on friendship ("How to Tell a Flatterer from a Friend").

[57] According to Cicero (*De Inventione*, 1.47), "A mind without *fides* cannot be relied on by friends." Plutarch ("Advice on Marriage," 96E) similarly notes: "But real friendship seeks a stable, firm, unchanging character of single place and habit."

[58] Unfortunately, a preoccupation with the text critical problem in 2:7 directs the exegete's attention away from the rhetorical development of the text. What is at stake is Paul's portrayal of the missionaries as faithful or unchanging across a period of time.

On the pedagogical role of the ancient nurse (*nutrix*), K. R. Bradley says "the evidence of literature, deriving from authors of very diverse geographical origins, complements the evidence of inscriptions, and it cannot be doubted that the *nutrix* was often an integral part of a child's life from birth to maturity" (1991:26). Cf. Livy, 3.44-48; Dion., *Roman Antiquities*, 11.28-29; Pliny, *Letters*, 6.3,5.16.3. On the pedagogical roles of both the nurse and the father, see Malherbe 1990:386.

[59] As we shall see in 2:1-12, Paul also uses "the true philosopher vs. the false philosopher" typology and "the rustic *vs.* the urbanite" typology. Again, the purpose is the same—to heighten the *ethos* of the missionaries, thus, enhancing the virtuous quality of the congregation.

[60] Although Roscio is drawn in the image of a rustic, his land-

NOTES TO CHAPTER 2

holdings were expansive. See Vasaly 1993:168-169.

[61] In his *Pro Caelio*, Cicero takes the opposite approach. Instead of castigating urbanites, he "treats the audience throughout the speech as urbane and sophisticated individuals, who can see through the appearances and masks that might fool a mere spectator" (Vasaly 1993:181).

[62] For more on this contrast, see Libanius' *Progymnasmata*, 349-360; Quintilian, 2.4.24; 9.3.99.

[63] On toil and virtue, see, for example, Diogenes Laertius, 6.2. On the virtuous value of dutiful toil in the *Aeneid*, see Goins 1993: 375-84. For an excellent discussion of self-sufficiency as a sign of ethical virtue in the writings of Homer, Hesiod, Plato, Xenophon of Athens, Aristotle, the Epicureans, Cynics and Stoics, see Most 1989: 127-128. Cf., for example, Epicurus, 2.82; 4.128. Also, compare Arthur W. H. Adkins who asserts that the "keynote of *arete* [virtue] is self-sufficiency" (1963:44).

[64] Representatives of this position are: Robert Jewett 1986; Abraham Malherbe 1987; Ronald Hock 1980. Both Jewett and Hock clearly insist that Paul was a handworker (Jewett, 120) or artisan (Hock, 27, 35), but Malherbe's position is ambiguous. On the one hand, he says that Paul worked "his trade in the company of fellow manual laborers" (33). On the other hand, he notes that "Paul's decision to engage in manual labor was a sacrifice, for he did not belong to the working class" (55). Linking 1 Thess 2:9-12 and 2 Thess 3:6-12, Jewett contends that Paul's audience at Thessalonica consisted of "employees or self-employed laborers," (120) or, more specifically "artisans" (cf. 121, 129). Hock, whose interest lies in identifying the context of *Paul's ministry* rather than *his audience*, does not explicitly call the congregation manual laborers. Yet, he persists in categorizing Paul's congregation as "urban poor" (45, 46, 47) to whom Paul recommended the occupation of manual labor in accordance with the recommendations of Greco-Roman philosophers (47). Malherbe specifically calls the congregation "manual laborers (56).

[65] Antisthenes, as with most Cynics, had this view of toil. See Diogenes Laertius, 6.2. Cf. Plutarch, *Lives*, 4.5.

[66] In Seneca's *Ad Helviam*, the ancestors worked in simplicity with "their own hand" (10.7) and Manius Curius, one of Rome's early leaders, cooked "with his own hand" (10.8). Both utopian examples are set in contrast to the toil of Seneca's past or present contemporaries, especially the insatiable Gaius Caesar (cf. 10.4).

[67] One religious tradition, for which there is archaeological information in Thessalonica, was the Cabiric cult, but it was not exclusively the cult of the artisans. Cabirus was also the guardian of sailors and was believed to bring good luck in peril. See Nock 1941:577; cf. Barclay 1993:519 n. 24.

[68] Paul's understanding of prestige appears to be similar to Seneca's Stoic concept of glory in that both allow for the recognition

of glory as long as one does not pursue it. On Seneca's understanding of glory, see Newman 1988:145-59.

NOTES TO CHAPTER THREE: DETERMINING THE GENRE

[1] Poe's tales ("The Purloined Letter," "The Mystery of Marie Roget," and "The Rue Morgue") were written between 1841-1845. For more on Poe as a progenitor of the classic detective fiction, notwithstanding a few ancient forebears (Sophocles included), see Lock 1991:26.

[2] Christopher Clausen (1984:116) also notes that other Victorian writers (Disraeli, Dickens, Tennyson, Arnold and Huxley) were aware of the unrest.

[3] According to Christopher Clausen, "Generally speaking, Holmes finds aristocrats or industrialists unappealing, but he never says a word against either aristocracy or industrialism" (1984:115). Cf. Kaemmel 1983:58; Lock 1991:7.

[4] On postmodernism, see Hutcheon 1988.

[5] In studies of other Pauline texts, the debate about the "rhetorical genre" rages on. Hans Dieter Betz (1975:355-59; 1979:15) views Galatians as apologetic, while George Kennedy (1984:144-46), Robert Hall (1987) and Joop Smit (1989) see it as deliberative; Burton Mack (1990:61) and Duane F. Watson (1989) see parts of 1 Corinthians (chapter 9 and 8:1-11:1 respectively) as epideictic while Margaret Mitchell (1989:17) views the entire letter as deliberative.

[6] According to Aristotle (*Rhetoric* 1.3.1), there are three species of rhetoric: deliberative, forensic and epideictic. Deliberative rhetoric is used to exhort or dissuade an audience about a future action. Forensic rhetoric seeks to persuade the audience to accuse or defend a past action. Epideictic rhetoric seeks to persuade an audience to praise or blame an action in the present.

[7] On using genre as a beginning point for interpretation, see Ralph Cohen (1985:227) who asserts that "genre is the organizing principle for rendering artistic material most available for sociological analysis."

[8] Kenneth Burke (1953:31) defines form as "the creation of an appetite in the mind of the auditor, and the adequate satisfying of that appetite."

[9] Kenneth Burke's terminology here is appropriate, for he speaks of Aristotle's rhetorical genres (deliberative, forensic and epideictic) as "forms-in-the-large" (1969:69-78).

[10] It is well known that Isocrates used "praise and blame" *topoi* for deliberative purposes in epideictic speeches (Grant and Kitzinger, eds., 1988:1094). On the use of these *topoi* in each of the comprehensive genres, see Aristotle, *Rhetoric*, 3.16.11; *Ad Herennium*, 3.8.15;

Cicero, *De Inventione*, 1-57; cf. 2.52.157ff; Quintilian, *Inst.*, 3.4.6-16.

[11] Given that *proxima genera* can share *topoi*, one cannot simply determine a genre type on the basis of a single *topos* (cf. Mitchell 1989:16, n. 41). Instead, one must consider the exigence and the strategic use of all of the *topoi* to determine the specific genre.

[12] While most scholars would agree with Abraham Malherbe (1987:74) that the self-description parts of 1 Thessalonians (particularly 2:1-12) do not the reflect the forensic (or apologetic) species, there is still no consensus with respect to the other two species. George Kennedy (1984:142) and Bruce Johanson (1987:41) assert that the entire letter is a deliberative one, but George Lyons (1985:177-221), Wilhelm Wuellner (1986:7) and Robert Jewett (1986:72) assert that it belongs to the epideictic species. Note, moreover, that while Jewett does not call 1 Thessalonians forensic, he does assert that the self-commending section in 2:1-12 depicts a situation of conflict between Paul and some of the Thessalonians (103).

[13] Again, I must note that I use the term "Hellenistic" in a cultural sense, and not in a political or ethnic sense.

[14] We would do well to follow the advice of Heikki Koskenniemi (1956:62), John L. White (1986:190), and Stanley Stowers (1988:81) —each of whom states that both manuals (Pseudo-Demetrius' *Typoi Epistolikoi* [c. 3rd century BCE–3rd century CE] and Pseudo-Libanius' *Epistolimaioi Characteres* [c. 4-6th century CE]) reflect not 21 or 41 letter "types," but a variety of circumstances to which a letter would need to be addressed.

[15] On the admonitory function of panegyric (thanksgivings and praise literature), see Barr 1981:22; Stadter 1987:253. Also, note that Robert Jewett's motivation—at least in part—for selecting the thanksgiving letter as a model for 1 Thessalonians is simply that this genre fits the "purpose and character of 1 Thessalonians as found in standard commentaries and introductions" (1986:72).

[16] On maxims (traditional, taken-for-granted arguments), see Aristotle (*Rhetoric*, 2.21.2,16), who places maxims in his discussion of the common proofs in formal logical reasoning, thus granting them a genre-transcending role. On reminders, note that Abraham Malherbe regards *oidate* ("all of you know") statements in 1 Thessalonians as paraenetic reminders (1972:13). Yet, such statements were standard fare in the rhetorical manipulation of any audience (cf. Aristotle, *Rhetoric*, 3.7.7).

[17] For the few scholarly writings which explore consolatory traditions, see the section in this chapter entitled "1 Thessalonians as a Letter of Consolation."

[18] See further Gustav Staehlin (1968) on *parakaleō*. Also note that *parakaleō* can mean both to console and to exhort and it is often associated with *paramytheisthe* (see Staehlin [1968] on *paramytheomai*). Also, see Plutarch's *Consolatio ad Apollonium*, 102B.

[19] C. E. Manning notes that consolatory writings were a "natural literary development of the Hellenistic age when the prime concern of philosophy was to equip the individual to meet the changes and chances of life" (1981:12).

[20] On Cicero's view of the value of philosophy in eradicating grief as well as other disorders, see *Tusculan Disputations*, 4.38 (cf. Gregg 1975:81).

[21] Gustav Staehlin (1968:783) mentions clinics as a third form of consolation other than visits and letters, but the extant texts from antiquity said little about them (unless clinics are deemed tantamount to the philosophical schools themselves). At any rate, clinics do not seem relevant in a study of 1 Thessalonians.

[22] See Cicero, *Tusculan Disputations*, 3.34; Seneca, *Ira*, 2.10.7; Dio Chrysostom, *Oration* 8.8. On Plutarch's use of the medical model, see Plutarch, *Consolatio ad Apollonium*, 102B.

[23] As Mary Edmond Fern notes, "Greek philosophers in their efforts to define the soul made some subtle and delicate analyses which revealed that the soul, just as the body, had its 'diseases;' among these they considered sorrow and the various forms of distress. After the diagnosis of the evil they applied themselves to the cure" (1941:3; and see Stowers 1986:142).

[24] In the speech of Achilles to Priam, who weeps for his son Hector (*Iliad*, 24.549-51), consolation is spoken of as *paramythētikos logos*. Also, cf. Telemachus' consolatory words to his mother (*Odyssey*, 1.345-355). Cf. Gregg 1975:2.

For more on the beginning of the consolatory tradition, see Atkinson 1985:867. Unfortunately, Crantor's work *On Grief* has not remained intact but subsequent authors in antiquity (e.g., Plutarch, Cicero and Seneca) quoted from it. See, for example, Cicero, *Academica*, 2.135. Cf. Gregg 1975:11.

[25] Among the Cynics, the works of Antisthenes, Diogenes of Sinope and perhaps Teles are excellent examples; and among the Stoics, so are the works of Chrysippus of Soli, Posidonius and Panaetius. Among the Epicureans, note Lucretius, *De Rerum Natura*, 783ff; and see Cicero's discussion of the contributions of both the Epicureans and the Cyrenaic Cynics on the topic of grief (Cicero, *Tusculan Disputations*, 3.13). Also, see Gregg 1975:10-11; cf. Atkinson 1985:867.

[26] On the evolution of the ancient consolations, Phillip H. De Lacy and Benedict Einarson (1959:577) assert that "the pattern for the philosophical consolations of the Hellenistic age was set by Crantor. Behind Crantor there was a long literary tradition, extending from Homer through tragedy and the public funeral orations at Athens." See further Seckler 1982:134. On the structure, see Ziolkowski 1981:57. For an ancient discussion on funeral orations and consolatory speeches, see Menander, *Rhetores*, 413.5–414.8.10.

[27] In part, however, consolations are indebted to the antagonistic

Greek public funeral oration for their antithetical character (see Poulakos 1990:182).

[28] A note is in order here about ancient suicide. However morally reprehensible it may appear to us today, it was not necessarily viewed that way in ancient times, at least not by Seneca. For a sterling discussion of suicide, including the differing positions of Stoics like Seneca and Epictetus, see Droge and Tabor 1992:34.

[29] The more formal consolations of Cicero and Seneca include Cicero's *Consolatio* (a lost work the content of which is likely preserved in his *Tusculan Disputations*) and Seneca's *Ad Marciam*, *Ad Helviam* and *Ad Polybium* (see Gregg 1975:35-41). Note that whereas some scholars doubt that Seneca wrote *Consolatio ad Polybium*, Atkinson (861-864) has provided evidence to show that this work is an authentic letter (treatise) written by Seneca *c.* 43 or 44 CE.

Both Cicero and Seneca also wrote letters of consolation, as opposed to formal consolatory treatises. See Cicero's letter to Titius (*Ad Familiares*, 5.16) and Seneca's consolatory letter-essays (*Epistles* 63, 93 and 99), all of which are addressed to Lucilius. Cicero also wrote *Somnium Scipionis*, a vision report which includes a number of consolatory *topoi*.

[30] See Malherbe 1983:254-256; 1987:57; Stowers 1986:145; Martin and Phillips 1978:413. Between the publication of my dissertation and this present study, I have read two separate studies treating conventions of consolation in 1 Thessalonians. In one, Karl P. Donfried (1989:247, 259, 260) briefly alludes to consolation material, but his work depends too heavily on Acts for a determination of the exigence prompting Paul to write 1 Thessalonians. In the other, Abraham Malherbe (1990:382) notes that two types of exhortation—consolation (*paramythia*) and admonition (*nouthesia*)—might profit from further treatment in New Testament commentaries. Moreover, while Malherbe is correct in noting in the article that consolatory *topoi* can serve a paraenetic purpose, we have already seen that paraenetic *topoi* can likewise serve consolatory purposes as in the funeral orations; and so can admonition as in the case of *nouthetemata* in Plutarch's *Consolatio ad Apollonium* [102B]. (Note Paul's *noutheteite* [5:14], a cognate form of Plutarch's *nouthetemata*.) The point is that the presence of *topoi* alone cannot determine genre. One has to consider the *exigence* and the *overall goal* of the letter, and the estimation deduced and noted here and in the succeeding chapter is that the *exigence* of 1 Thessalonians primarily is Paul's abrupt separation and the *overall strategy* is to neutralize the grief caused by that separation with arguments coopted from the consolatory tradition. Of course, if Malherbe understands exhortation in a broad modalistic way—somewhere between comprehensive rhetorical genres and epistolary genres, then, his argument could still be persuasive. My retort, then, is simply that my quest for the audience is a quest for a specifi-

cally nuanced *typical situation* that permits a closer viewing of Paul's congregation at Thessalonica.

[31] For example, Stanley Stowers asserts that "Paul's attempt to comfort the grieving Thessalonians clearly follows ancient consolation to a point. His appeal to the resurrection, however, introduces specifically Christian grounds of consolation that would be central to later Christian consolation" (1986:145).

[32] On Cicero's avoidance of "hackneyed consolatory" conventions in his letter of consolation to Titius (discussed in *Ad. Fam.*, 5.16), see Weinrib 1990:289.

[33] Seneca (*Ad Marciam*, 2.1) testifies to this freedom in his consolation to Marcia: "I am aware that all those who wish to give to give anyone admonition commonly begin with precepts, and end with examples. But it is desirable at times to alter this practice."

[34] Menander of Laodicea (3rd century CE), for example, divides the consolatory speech into three parts: *laudatio*, *lamentatio* and *consolatio*. See Menander, *Rhetores*, 413.5-414.30. For more on the inclusion of a laudation section in the lament in an actual letter of consolation, see Gregg 1975:54. On the formal unit related to the author's knowledge of the misfortune, see Gregg 1975:58.

[35] On the influence of the ancient diatribal mode of writing, see Scourfield 1993:17; Fern 1941:205.

[36] Note how Polycharmus repeatedly comforts his friend Chaereas whose melancholy constantly peaks to a suicidal level (Chariton, *Chaereas and Callirhoe*, 3.6.8; 4.4.1; 5.2.6; 8.1.6).

[37] In Ovid's consolatory elegies, Ovid acknowledges the mutual duty of remembering each other in times of distress (*Tristia*, 1.8.11; *Pontiques*, 3.5.37-38). See Nagle 1980:41.

[38] My answer to the question of whether the deaths had already taken place or were simply expected by Paul must await the next chapter.

[39] Note Abraham Malherbe's assertion that consolation "was offered not only at death but on the occasion of all misfortunes that caused grief" (1986:82). Moreover, according to Robert C. Gregg, the philosophers "developed arguments designed for the consolation of the whole spectrum of human misfortunes—exile, destruction of *patria*, physical disability, and that subject of the vast majority of such writing, death" (1975:4).

[40] The term orphan is also used by Seneca to explain how his niece would feel about his exile from her. To his mother, he says: "Hold to your bosom Novatilla, who so soon will present you with great-grandchildren, whom I had so transferred to myself, had so adopted as my own, that in losing me she may well seem to be an orphan although her father is still living." Seneca, *Ad Helviam*, 18.7.

[41] That the father and wetnurse images are pedagogical roles within the philosophical coinage of ancient times has been shown by Abraham Malherbe (1970:203-18).

[42] Tiberius, the emperor, is praised, moreover, in *Ad Marciam*, for a type of virtuous quality (*magna pietas*, 4.2) characteristic of Marcia as well (4.2). As Jane Bellemore (1992:222) explains, it is evident that this letter was written after Tiberius had redeemed himself in the eyes of Marcia, for (as Tacitus reveals in his *Annals*, 6.47), Tiberius actually played a role in the demise of Marcia's father, Cordus. Other figures praised in the letter (treatise) are Marcellus (Augustus' nephew, 2.3), Augustus (15.2) and all the Caesars (15.1).

[43] Note Plutarch's condemnation of flatterers in his consolation to Apollonius. *Ad Apollonium*, 117F.

[44] On the issue of self-consolation, see Stowers 1986:145; also Martin and Phillips 1978:403. On Seneca's advice to Helvia, see Seneca, *Ad Helviam*, 18.5-19.4. Furthermore, note the similarity between the comforting charges in 1 Thess 4:18 and 5:11 and the one in the following papyrus letter cited by Abraham Malherbe (1986:82): "Be of good courage! I sorrowed and wept over the departed one as I did over Didymus. I did everything that was fitting, and so did all of my household, Epaphroditus and Thermythion and Philion and Apollonius and Plantas. But, nevertheless, against such things one can do nothing. Therefore, comfort one another. Farewell."

[45] Note that in Plutarch's letter of consolation to his wife, he praises her behavior and encourages her to continue in that way. See Plutarch *Consolatio ad Uxorem*, 608F-610C; also, Martin and Phillips 1978:412.

[46] Given the audience-oriented approach of this study, several words are in order about apocalypticism and Paul's auditors. First, like Hans Dieter Betz, I assert that the issues of apocalypticism were not the concerns of Jews alone in the Hellenistic world. As Betz notes, "We have to free ourselves from the idea of treating apocalypticism as an isolated and purely inner-Jewish phenomenon. Rather we must learn to understand apocalypticism as a peculiar manifestation within the entire course of Hellenistic oriental syncretism" (1969:152).

Second, in this work I am not interested in establishing apocalypticism as a central framework for Paul's thought, though I think Pauline studies has profited immeasurably from the writings of Richard Kabisch and Albert Schweitzer, who almost a century ago ushered in the shift in Pauline interpretation from the ethical tradition of German liberal piety to a Jewish apocalyptic context. For more on the history of Pauline interpretation from the late nineteenth century to the present, see Kuck 1992:1-37.

Third, my interest largely lies then in the effect which Paul's apocalyptic rhetoric had on one specific community, Paul's congregation at Thessalonica. I speak now especially about his distinction between "sons of light" and "sons of darkness" (5:5; cf.1QM); his judgment against living like Gentile idolaters or oppressors (2:14-16; 4:5; cf. *Sibylline Oracles*, 3.34–35.601-34; Judith) and his belief that a series of end-time afflictions would proceed the day of the Lord (3:3; 5:3; cf.2 and 4 Maccabees).

[47] Note the near fatalistic terms in 1 Thess 3:3-4: "You yourselves know that this is to be our 'lot' (keimetha). For when we were with you, we told you beforehand that we 'were' (mellomen) to suffer affliction."

[48] Speaking of the ancient consolatory view of death as a gift, Martin and Phillips (1978:403) note, "The gods' judgment about the relative values of life and death is shown by the stories of their awarding death to men for great virtue." Cf. Seneca who says "those who are treated most kindly by Nature are those whom she removes early to a place of safety" (Ad Marciam, 22.3).

[49] The quote comes from Paul Brooks Duff (1991:82) who lists as examples of this view: 1 Macc 6:12-13; Acts 5; 12:19-23; Josephus, Antiquities, 19.8.2. I would add Diodorus (Library of History,35.2.47), who shows the popularity of the belief when he says: "the great mass of humanity abstain from evil-doing only because of the penalties of the law and the retribution that comes from the gods."

[50] On God as a father or teacher, Seneca asserts that "The sage is God's friend, his pupil, imitator, and true offspring." See De Providentia, 1.5. In the same text (2.6), Seneca declares: "Toward good men God has the mind of a father; he cherishes for them a manly love."

[51] On the wise man as one called by God to be a witness, see Epictetus, Discourses, 1.29.46, 47; 2.139.

[52] As Epictetus (Discourses, 4.8.30-32) says about the ideal Cynic, "Such is the way of the Cynic who is deemed worthy of the sceptre and diadem of Zeus, and says, 'That you may see yourselves, O men, to be looking for happiness and serenity, not where it is, but where it is not, behold, God has sent me to you as an example. . . But see whose work it is, it is the work of Zeus, or of him whom Zeus deems worthy of this service'."

[53] Speaking about the wise man, Epictetus (Discourses, 3.22.56) says: "And is he not persuaded that whatever of these hardships he suffers (paschē), it is Zeus that is exercising him?"

[54] Note Seneca's claim that "God does not make a spoilt pet of a good man; he tests him, burdens him, and fits him for his service" (Providentia, 1.4). Cf. Epictetus, Discourses, 4.1.176.

[55] In the first six books of the Aeneid (the so-called Odyssean half), Aeneas' labors are trials of endurance similar to the trials of Hercules. See Goins 1993:375-84, esp., 379-381; cf. McGushin, 1964: 234; Bowra 1933:11.

[56] In the novels, the leading characters are propelled throughout the oikoumenē—often a series of agōnes (struggles or trials)—among successively greater networks of power. Their successful, albeit toilsome, journeys from private spheres to larger, more public, arenas are

strategically designed to demonstrate both the ultimate safe-keeping power of a particular deity and the abiding fidelity of the protagonists, despite increasing instability and catastrophic reversals. See further, on fidelity in hardships as a theme of the novels, Hock 1988:134.

[57] In 2:4, Paul speaks of himself as approved (*dedokimasmetha*). Compare Seneca's claim that "God hardens, reviews, and disciplines those whom he approves, whom he loves." *De Providentia*, 4.16. Also, note Plutarch's laudation of exiled wise persons as "most approved (*dokimotatoi*)." *On Exile*, 605B. On Paul's conception of being approved in 1 Thessalonians, see Sampley 1991:65.

[58] Cf. *Ad Apollonium*, 120B; Pseudo-Ovid, *Ad Liviam*, 209-216. See Martin and Phillips 1978:402.

[59] In consolatory letters, death is often euphemistically called sleep. See Plutarch, *Consolatio ad Apollonium*, 107D; cf. Stowers 1986:145.

[60] On stability (*stabilem*) as the goal in Seneca's consolation to Marcia, see *Ad Marciam*, 5.6.

[61] Obviously, the philosophical precepts were not homogeneous, for the various philosophical groups or movements differed both in their opinions about the soul's composition and the degree to which emotions were appropriate (Martin and Phillips 1978:404). Even within a particular branch of philosophy, differing opinions evolved over time. So, while the early Stoics' (e.g., Zeno and Chrysippus) monistic psychology supported their view of *apatheia* toward all emotions, as in the tradition of the harsh Cynics, the later Stoics, because they were influenced by the humanism of the Middle Stoic and neo-Platonic Posidonius, returned to Plato's tripartite view of the soul, thus conceding that the soul consisted of three parts (a rational element and two irrational components: a highspirited element and an appetitive one) rather than one and thus allowing for some emotion.

Of course, our interest lies the cultural literacy of the first century, when philosophers and philosophical movements were generally eclectic about matters of grief. Hence, we need not detail any more of the basic or subtle differences among the various groups; what is common to all, however, is the goal of "subjecting man's [sic] emotional life, uncontrolled, unpredictable, and unconstructive, to the rule of reason" (Martin and Phillips 1978:404). And for this goal, precepts were an invaluable resource.

For more on the differences among the groups, see Gregg 1975: 104-119; Manning 1981:33-34.

[62] On precepts formulated as maxims for the purpose of overcoming obstacles, see Seneca, *Ep.* 13.1.

[63] It must be stated that words about fortification were not the exclusive domain of philosophers. As Victoria Tietze notes: "We must not forget that that imagery is also embedded in colloquial language often in the form of proverbs" (1985:93).

[64] The same could be said for his gnomic precepts on joy (5:16; cf.2:19; 3:9) and prayer (5:17; cf.1:2; 3:9).

[65] The diction of misjudgments (or false opinions) was a part of the philosophical *koinē* of Paul's day. It is with little wonder then that Seneca (*Ad Marciam*, 1.19) can say to Marcia, "What tortures us, therefore, is an opinion, and every evil is only as great as we have reckoned it to be."

[66] As I will explain in the next chapter, I differ from some commentators who think that Paul was admonishing his auditors for misconstruing what he had said about the day of the Lord at the beginning of his ministry to the Thessalonians. Rather, I see Paul's remarks in 5:1ff as reminders intended to habituate the congregation in correct judgments about changing circumstances. On the habituation of correct judgments in the consolations, see Plutarch, *Ad Uxorem*, 611A.

[67] As Martin and Phillips explain anticipation of suffering in consolatory literature, "Training the mind in the thought that nothing is unexpected makes grief easier to bear when it comes" (1978:403). On the anticipation of misfortunes, note that Cicero says "we have on the tip of our tongues as a rule the words 'nothing should seem unexpected'" (*Tusculan Disputations*, 3.23.55). Also, Epictetus says: "And again, go now to one man and to another. Then, if some one of those things happens which are called undesirable, immediately the thought that it was not unexpected will be the first thing to lighten the burden" (*Discourses*, 3.24.103-4). Also, cf. Seneca, *Epistle*, 24.15 and *Epistle*, 91.4.

NOTES TO CHAPTER FOUR: RECONSTRUCTING THE RHETORIC

[1] In her reflections about *Song of Solomon*'s twist on classical myths, Morrison notes: "I want to subvert his [the reader's] traditional comfort so that he may experience an unorthodox one: that of being in the company of his own solitary imagination" (1984:387). Helen Mary Lock (1991:4) suggests that the works of several African-American writers (Toni Morrison, Ishmael Reed and Ralph Ellison) frustrate the formulas and conventions of detective fiction, and thereby these authors "challenge reader expectation, and . . . force a re-examination of the assumptions on which the genre was established."

[2] For more on rhetorical exigence, see A. Miller 1972; cf. Bitzer 1968. As I stated in Chapter One, I have taken into consideration Richard Vatz' critique (1973) of Lloyd F. Bitzer's concept of the rhetorical situation, namely, that any speaker has the ability to control how a situation is perceived through his or her description of that situation.

[3] Note the quotation from Euripides used in Plutarch's consolation to Apollonius (*Ad Apollonium*, 702A): "For divers ills are remedies

diverse: The kindly speech of friends for one in grief." Also, note that Seneca (*Ad Polybium*, 7.11f) tells Polybius to turn to the emperor Claudius for consolation. Cf. Seneca's *Ad Helviam*, 18.5-19.4.

[4] According to William Dowling, all of the letters of Paul, like the letters of the Epicureans, were designed to "summon into existence an alternative community in periods when an older order is thought to be in a state of disintegration" (1991:38).

[5] As John R. Wilson asserts: "As an ethical principle, *philia* represents a continuum of attachment that extends in a stable system of relationships from the self to one's immediate family and friends and then outwards to one's *polis* and one's race" (1989:151).

[6] As D. A. Russell puts it, "On the one hand it [*philia*] denotes any kind of affinity or close association; on the other, like the Latin *amicitia*, it implies an overt relationship of duties and expectations which may, but need not, involve a warm feeling of affection" (1973: 93).

[7] Plutarch (*De Amic. Mult.*, 96D) says that "friendship comes into being through likeness." According to John R. Wilson (1989:151), "shared attachment or *philia* also involves shared hostility or *echthra*, which can be as permanent as *philia*." In Chariton, Polycharmus is Chaereas' true friend (*philos pistos* 8.8.12). Not only do the two men wish to be sold into slavery together (3.7.3), but Polycharmus even wishes to die with Chaereas (4.2.14).

[8] According to Plutarch (*De Amic. Mult.*, 96A,B), "Enmities follow close upon friendships, and are interwoven with them, inasmuch as it is impossible for a friend not to share his friend's wrongs or disrepute or disfavor."

[9] Plutarch (*De Amic. Mult.*, 95A) highlights the unity of friends and the beneficence between them when he says: "For friendship draws persons together and unites them and keeps them united in a close fellowship by means of a continual association and mutual acts of kindness." Alan Mitchell (1992), writing on the friendship summary statements in Acts (2:44-47; 4:32-37), sheds light on the economic aspects of ancient friendship.

[10] Several familial kinds of associations are evoked in the diction of 1 Thessalonians: 1) God as Father (1:1; 1:3; 3:11, 13); 2) Jesus (1:10) and the Thessalonians (and the missionaries) as sons (5:5); 3) the missionaries and the Thessalonians as brothers; 4) Paul as father (2:11, 12); and 5) the Thessalonians as children (2:7, 8).

[11] In 4:9-12, Paul uses the word "brother" three times as a way of solidifying the congregation's *philia* network in opposition to the "outsiders" (*tous exō*, 4:12). Later, in 4:13, Paul uses the term "brothers" in opposition to the term "the rest" (*hoi loipoi*). Furthermore, he opposes the "they" of 5:3 ("they say" ([*legōsin*]) to "brothers" (*adelphoi*) in 5:4.

[12] As David Aune has noted, by 50 CE Christianity as a whole

had an identity problem because "unlike other ancient Mediterranean religions, it had ceased to remain tied to a particular ethnic group (i.e., it had increasingly looser relations to Judaism)" (1986:137). In fact, he goes on to say, a number of Jewish Christians "apparently advocated that Christians (whether Jews or Gentiles) ignore or regard as nonessential the traditional signs of Jewish social and religious identity (circumcision, Sabbath and festival observance, dietary restrictions, and the wearing of religious paraphernalia, such as phylacteries and fringes)."

[13] According to Pheme Perkins, "Ability to surmount affliction is evidence for the 'power' which the apostle and his converts have received from the true God (1:5-9)" (1989:330). She also notes that the Qumran writings reflect an interest in the power of endurance as well (e.g., 1QH 2:23-25). In 1 Thessalonians, excessive force is wielded by some of the Jews and the congregation's compatriots (2:14ff).

[14] The view of limited emotions originates in the West with Plato (cf. *The Republic*, 10.603-4) and is often associated with his student, Crantor, who argued that the absence of emotions indicated a deficiency and thus was just as unnatural as an excess of emotions. For a fuller discussion, see Gregg 1975:83-89. That Seneca concedes to limited emotions at all may reflect his indebtedness to the postulates of the Middle Stoic and neo-Platonic Posidonius.

[15] At this point, Seneca (*Ad Marciam*, 7.1) notes, "But false opinion has added something more to our grief than Nature has prescribed."

[16] Obviously, any rhetorical analysis involves circularity of argument because both the rhetorical *dispositio* and the rhetorical exigence are primarily determined by an interpreter's reading of the text. The circularity is lessened somewhat by the generic constraints in that the interpretation of the text now rests in part with the constraints of several other similar texts.

[17] Not to pay attention to structure is to invite traditional readings which often begin interpretations in the middle or at the end of a text as if the preceding material mattered little for setting the stage for what follows.

[18] Joachim Classen (1992:343) suggests caution in using *dispositio* rhetorical theory.

[19] Mary Edmond Fern (1941:39) suggests that Seneca follows this basic plan in his consolation essays (*Ad Marciam, Ad Helviam, Ad Polybium*) and in Epistle 23.

[20] Note the repetition of the term "one other" (*allēlous*) in 4:9, 18; 5:11, 13.

[21] Recent analyses of 1 Thessalonians by George Kennedy (1984), Robert Jewett (1986) and Wilhelm Wuellner (1986) have already noted the verses which correspond to the various parts of Paul's rhetorical design. None of these scholars, however, has shown

how such a design is perceived from the text itself and none of them has shown explicitly any other justification for their rhetorical divisions except for their sense of how certain verses seem to perform the functions of a certain part of the rhetorical design. Note that Bruce C. Johanson (1987:5-6) agrees that the present rhetorical analyses offer no explicit justification for their divisions.

For the most part, the present writer agrees with parts of each of these scholars' adumbrations, but some emendations will be made in light of what we have discovered from our previous analysis of the generic model for Thessalonians. Admittedly, moreover, my analysis of the opening of 1 Thessalonians will require extended discussion, but a lengthy analysis will help orient the modern reader to the early cues readily available to Paul's authorial audience.

22 On the orientation of the literary techniques towards the spoken word, see Parunak 1981:154. On the literary techniques as tools for the memory and for the organization of material, see John W. Welch's introduction (1981:8-15, esp. 12).

23 The definition for a ring composition is taken from Joanna Dewey (1980:32-34; see Moskalew 1982:122-23). To my knowledge, the ancient rhetors never recorded the Latin or Greek equivalents for chiasmus, inclusios and ring compositions. Their interest in repetition, as shown in the last chapter, however, suggests that the nomenclature is not as important as the presence of a variety of repetitive forms, all of which functioned to amplify and organize an argument.

24 On the peroration (the closing of an argument), see *Rhetorica ad Alexandrum*, 34; 36.15-22; Cicero, *De Inventione*, 1.53-56; Cicero, *De Oratore*, 34.122; *Ad Herennium*, 2.30.47–31.50.

25 The variations found in recent analyses of the exordium of 1 Thessalonians is sobering. George Kennedy (1984:142) asserts that the exordium is found in 1:2-10, Wilhelm Wuellner (1986:1) suggests that it is found in 1:1-10, and Robert Jewett (1986:72-73) avers that it is found in 1:1-5.

26 C. E. Manning (1981:27) asserts that *Ad Marciam* 1.1-4, a section on Marcia's virtues, constitutes a *captatio benevolentiae*.

27 Cicero, *De Inventione*, 1.16.22; *Ad Herennium*, 1.5.1;5.8. Cf. *Ad Helviam* (1.1) where Seneca calls his mother the "best of mothers."

28 The participles are *poioumenoi*, "while doing," 1:2; *mnemoneuontes*, "while remembering," 1:3; and *eidotes*, "while knowing," 1:4.

29 Paul Ellingworth and Eugene Nida are on the mark when they describe "steadfastness" (*hypomonēs*) as "resisting or holding out against an enemy, especially over an extended period of time" (1969:7).

30 A. A. Long asserts that the "Stoics distinguished good men from others by reference to the consistency of their logos" (1986:177).

31 A number of ancient writers condemned charlatans whose words while wise in appearance, were not matched by deeds. See Philo, *Vit. Mos.*, 2.209-216; Dio Chrysostom, *Oration*, 4.28-39.

[32] Perhaps, as early as 1:5, it is difficult for us to see that *plerophoria polle* indicates full conviction or correct thinking in preparation for tests or struggles. Yet the authorial audience likely actualizes this understanding, especially when Paul later associates *polle* ("many") or one of its cognate forms with affliction (*thlipsei*, 1:6) and agony (*agoni*, 2:2).

[33] *Ad Marciam*, 1.5–1.8 "outlines the approach Seneca intends to take in dealing with Marcia" (Manning 1981:27). According to Mary Edmond Fern, in *Ad Helviam*, Seneca "announces the evil he wishes to cure and the treatment he intends to apply" (1941:65).

[34] Note the cognitive expressions used in 2:1-12: "you know" (2:1,2,5,11); "you remember" (2:9); and "you are witnesses" (2:10).

[35] According to Robert J. Newman, in ancient times, true imitation means that one understands "the act and its motivating virtue or impulse and that one approves it" (1988:150).

[36] Holland Hendrix's study of archaeology and eschatology at Thessalonica compellingly demonstrates that the phrase "peace and security" (5:3) referred to Roman imperial propaganda, a type of propaganda propagated in various media forms before the rise of Augustus and continuing after him in the Julio-Claudian and Flavian times (1991:112-13). Exactly how Paul treats the propaganda will have to wait until Chapter Five.

[37] As we shall see, moreover, the congregation's self-consolation does not simply help the congregation. It helps other believers and outsiders as well.

[38] On God as a benefactor, father, and protector of proselytes, see Philo, *Special Laws*, 1.300, 318, 309, respectively.

[39] As we shall soon see, however, the issue of death plays an illustrative role.

[40] That is, the missionaries showed their maturity in withstanding much agony *in Thessalonica* just as boldly as they did *in Philippi*.

[41] Boykin Sanders has noted that a frequent use of the idea of imitation in the Greco-Roman world was that of a teacher who "would portray the life and conduct of its venerated founder or other figures from the past as a principle or model for the behavior of its members" (1981:358). Along the same lines, Abraham Malherbe (1983:246) has noted the occurrence of an imitation motif in the exhortations of Paul's contemporaries, the Stoic and the Cynic philosophers. He has also noted that whereas the Stoics would point to a revered figure from the past, the Cynics asked their readers to imitate them or other contemporary worthy individuals. On imitation in consolatory works, see *Ad Polybium*, 17.1,2,6; *Ad Apollonium*, 119D.

[42] Plutarch (*Ad Uxorem*, 608F; 609D) uses the reports of others to laud the noble character of his wife.

[43] It is curious that Paul begins 2:13-16 with a word of thanks. I think he does so to recall his emphasis on the missionaries' recognition of the congregation's laudable *ethos*. Thus, 2:13ff collapses the issues

NOTES TO CHAPTER 4

of 1:3ff to signal Paul's recognition of the community's singular virtue. In so doing, he returns from 2:1-12, a panegyric on the missionaries, to more direct words about the congregation. At the same time, the repetition of *adialeiptos* (constantly) in 1:2 and 2:13 signals the missionaries' virtue, that is, their constancy in thanking God in all circumstances (cf. 5:18).

44 Again, note that the onus of the vituperative remarks is not actually against the Jews opposing the churches of Judea but rather against the Gentiles who, as blocking characters, are standing in the way of the work of habituation which even now is continued by the word of God (2:13) (cf. Patte 1983:127).

45 Among the several scholars agreeing that Paul uses 2:1-12 to distinguish himself from the street preachers of his day is Hans Dieter Betz, who says: "When Paul wrote 1 Thessalonians 2:3-12, he was . . . obliged to draw a sharp distinction between himself and the religious charlatans who fickled the Roman world. Such men had a reputation for raising funds for what were purported to be good causes, and then lining their own pockets" (1985:76). Cf. Ellingworth and Nida 1969:23; Lyons 1985:197.

46 Plutarch (*Ad Apollonium*, 117F) suggests that helpful persons "will not, for flattery (*kolakeian*), grieve with us and arouse our sorrows, but will endeavour to dispel our griefs through noble consolation."

47 On ancient nurses and their role in the maturation of children, see Bradley 1991:26. Cf. Livy, 3.44-48; Dion, *Roman Antiquities*, 11.28-29; Pliny, *Letters*, 6.3, 5.16.3.

48 On false philosophers as glory-seekers, see Lucian's *The Passing of Peregrinus*. Also note Cicero's *Somnium Scipionis*, a consolatory writing in which a grandfather (Scipio Africanus) tells his grandson to avoid ephemeral glory. See Fern 1941:22.

49 The final section drops the antithetical style but abounds in pedagogical imagery again to illustrate the model character of the missionaries' earlier encouragement, as well as to show the aim of the missionaries' teachings—that is, to help the congregation become what, for Paul, was now already a reality: God's worthy models (2:12), even in the face of persecution.

50 Paul's shift in pedagogical metaphors from nurse to father is designed to show the missionaries' steadfast and ongoing habituation of the congregation.

51 Letters of consolation also included *partitios*. See *Ad Marciam*, 1.19; *Ad Helviam*, 4.1.

52 The plural form of the word alone (*monoi*) indicates that Paul refers to himself and Silvanus (3:1).

53 As Judith M. Gundry Volf has noted: "Anticipating what his [Paul's] converts will mean for him at the parousia, Paul can view them in this light even presently. This thought prefaces Paul's recounting of his great concern for the stability of the Thessalonians' faith

which caused him to send Timothy to the afflicted Christians that he might 'establish and exhort you in your faith' (3:1-4)" (1990:265).

[54] Again, Paul gives thanks to show the consistency of the missionaries' virtues.

[55] Note Paul's repeated emphasis on joy (chara, 2:19; chara, 2:20; and chara hē chairomen, 3:9).

[56] A number of scholars (Jewett 1986:77); Malherbe 1987:30; Johanson 1987:187) view only 3:11-13 as a kind of partitio or hinge closing off the first half of the letter with a new section beginning in 4:1. As we have seen, however, there are form and content parallels between 2:17-20 and all of 3:9-13.

[57] Cf. Cicero (De Inventione, 1.22.31) who speaks of the partitio as "the matters which we intend to discuss . . . in a methodical way."

[58] Again, note Seneca's advice to Marcia: "What tortures us, therefore, is an opinion, and every evil is only as great as we have reckoned it to be." Ad Marciam, 1.19.

[59] The adverb loipon in 4:1 (often translated as "finally"), is a transitional marker indicating the final set of three large, interrelated structures in 1 Thessalonians. Coming immediately after the partitio, loipon suggests that the reader will not have to wait long before seeing some of the same elements which gave closure to the second amplification unit. Indeed, directly after the third unit, Paul's peroration (5:23-28) harks back to 3:9-13.

[60] While Bruce C. Johanson (1987:111-112) asserts that the last large unit of 1 Thessalonians is 4:1-5:24, I would mark 5:22 as the end of the unit because of the contrast between 5:22 and 5:23, that is, the contrast between an imperatival form and an intercessory form of discourse. Moreover, whereas the rhetorical question in 3:9,10 (especially with the use of "while praying" [deomenoi]) naturally leads one to expect the prayer in 3:11-13, no such introductory material precedes 5:23. Also, note that although Johanson argues that 4:1-5:24 is a chiastic pattern, his outline of words common to 4:1-12 and 5:12-24 does not take into account any of the words in 5:23-24. For more on the differences between 3:9-13 and 5:23, 24, see Wiles 1974:65.

[61] Consistency was a feature of the consolatory tradition. In his consolatory letter to Titius (Ad Fam., 5.16.5), Cicero writes "The fact is that you have ever proved yourself, both in public and in private life, to be such that you are bound to maintain your high character and obey the dictates of consistency."

[62] Martin Dibelius (1937:19), looking at 4:3-8, for example, saw Paul's injunctions simply as the stock sayings from Paul's contemporary moralists.

[63] Note that the plural pronoun "these" (4:6) refers to all of the injunctions.

[64] In each case, excessive force is wielded, which hurts others, and God retaliates.

[65] Because Paul uses the transitional marker *peri de* (often translated as "concerning") in 4:1, 9; 5:1, some scholars think Paul shifts his focus. Actually, Paul does not shift; he intensifies. On *peri de*, see M. Mitchell 1989a:229-256.

[66] Blass-Debrunner calls *epidiorthosis* "a correction which intensifies what has been said" (1961:262, sec. 495 [3]). Again, see *Ad Herrenium*, 4.26.36; cf. Quintilian, 9.1.30.

[67] On Plutarch's use of outsider (*exōthen*) language, see *Ad Uxorem*, 610C, 611. On the "good form" as a feature of the Greco-Roman moralist's understanding of virtue, see Gooch 1987:98.

[68] Malherbe (1987:104) comes dangerously close to this opinion. For opposing opinions, see Kloppenborg 1993:280.

[69] John S. Kloppenborg suggests that Paul's issue with the community is that "*philadelphia* not be exploited by those unwilling to work" (1993:273). Unfortunately, Kloppenborg's thesis is influenced by the "work" references in 2 Thessalonians 3:11,12.

[70] On toil, see *Ad Marciam*, 16.1; on constancy, see *Ad Helviam*, 5.5; on tests of endurance, see *Epistle*, 13:1-3; *Ad Marciam*, 5.5-6). On hardships—even death—as an indication of divine favor or love, see *Ad Apollonium*, 111B;119E.

[71] That is, in 5:12-22, Paul shows the congregation how to comfort each other and how to extend personalized, individuated care. See Malherbe 1990:388-389.

Among those to receive care, the "weak" (*asthenōn*) are especially difficult to help because they have not had much training. On this understanding of the weak, compare Plutarch (*Ad Apollonium*, 119D): "but others have not the ability to imitate them [the noble-minded] in practice because of that weakness [*astheneian*] of spirit which results from [a] lack of education."

[72] Note Seneca's advice to Helvia (*Ad Helviam*, 5.1): "External things are of slight importance, and can have no great influence in either direction [happiness or sadness]. Prosperity does not exalt the wise man, nor does adversity cast him down; for he has always endeavored to rely entirely upon himself, to derive all of his joy from himself."

[73] Paul does not spell out what the good (5:21) means, though he does set the good in opposition to evil (5:22). As J. Paul Sampley (54) asserts: "The maxim in 1 Thess 5:21 makes no effort to answer the question, Good with respect to what?" (1991:54). On the clarification of maxims through antithesis, see Bonner 1966:262.

[74] Cf. the soldier imagery in Plutarch (*Ad Uxorem*, 610D; *Ad Apollonium*, 103A.

[75] John Philip Mason (1989) summarizes the various scholarly positions on 4:13-18. Some scholars think that Paul was compelled to previous instructions which were insufficient (89). Others suggest that the congregation failed to "maintain or to apply belief in the resurrection" (93). Still, others conclude that the section was necessary be-

cause the congregation thought that those believers who were yet alive had "an advantage over the dead" (96).

[76] Plutarch uses the term "snatched up" several times (111D, 117B, 111C) in his letter to Apollonius. Cf. Malherbe 1983:255-256.

[77] We have previously observed Paul's use of *paralipsis* and *epidiorthosis* in 4:9-12.

[78] Cf. Livy 40,37,2. Also, note that in the Hebrew Bible, the wrath of God was associated with death (e.g., note Job's friends' interpretation of his children's death in Job 8:3,4).

[79] In ancient times, peace was understood as the end of a political state's internal strife, while security was related to protection from external forces. See Nutton 1978:210.

[80] On the affective function of the peroration, see *Rhetorica ad Alexandrum*, 20-21; Cicero, *De Inventione*, 1.52; Cicero, *De Oratore*, 2.19.80. On the peroration's amplificatory function, see *Rhetorica ad Alexandrum*, 34; 36.15-22; Cicero, *De Inventione*, 1.53-56; Cicero, *De Oratore*, 34.122; *Ad Herennium*, 2.30.47–31.50.

[81] I agree with George Kennedy that 5:24 should not be separated from 5:23, but should be seen as a part of a transitional shift from 5:22 to 5:23, because the explicit nature of the verb *poiesei* ("to do") in 5:24 is given in 5:23 ("to keep" [*tēretheiē*]). Also, the inclusion of 5:24 is affirmed by the use of nominative forms in both 5:23 ("God" [*ho theos*]) and 5:24 ("the one who calls" [*ho kalōn*]). Moreover, as G. P. Wiles (1974:65) asserts, 5:24 is an "'Amen' sentence giving an answering promise of fulfillment."

[82] Note that both Wilhelm Wuellner (1986:1) and Robert Jewett (1986:76) also assert that 5:23-28 is the peroration.

[83] On prayer in the consolations, see *Ad Polybium*, 13.1-3. The anthropology in 5:23 is best understood within the interpretive sphere of friendship. Paul's point is that the "life" of the entire *philia* network will be kept by God. See A. Mitchell 1992:267.

[84] Ancient magistrates often used cognate forms of the word "to keep" (*tēretheiē*) to show their desire "to watch over or protect the privileges of a given community" (Sherk 1969:193).

NOTES TO CHAPTER FIVE:
THE AUDIENCE AND EXTRA-TEXTUAL EVIDENCE

[1] Most of the information about King's speech is adapted from Martha Solomon 1993:66-84.

[2] George N. Dionisopoulos, Victoria J. Gallagher, Steven R. Goldzwig and David Zarefsky suggests that all of King's speeches up until his Vietnam War speech at Riverside Church reflected the American dissent tradition (1992:91-107). James Murphy (1990) traces the American dissent tradition (a.k.a. the jeremiad tradition) from the Whig party of the 18th century to Robert F. Kennedy.

[3] Informed by Bengt Holmberg's recent discussions (1990) on the problems of measuring the social level of early Christian groups, I prefer the term "social standing" to "social status" or "class" because the latter two expressions evoke a modern and Western economic valence. Occasionally, however, to avoid repetitive diction or to treat precisely the reflections of other scholars, I am forced to use all three terms.

[4] Note Wayne Meeks' discussion of how the "typical" Christian could have "had houses, slaves, the ability to travel, and other signs of wealth" (1983:73).

[5] To date, no systematic archaeological work has been done on Thessalonica. See Jewett 1986:114.

[6] On the agora with two *insulae*, see Vickers 1976: "Thessalonike."

[7] On the different types of people dwelling in the *insulae*, note that Frank E. Brown avers that the architects of the Roman Empire worked with "ready inventiveness" and "in blocks up to five or six stories high they combined quarters for every degree of the great middle class, from the stately, ground-floor town apartments of the well-to-do to the garret flats of the less favored" (1979:39). Also, in light of the problem of increasing population in that time, the "so-called middle-class" housing and the mansions of wealthy persons were set in contiguity (A. G. McKay 1975:85). Note further that McKay (214-215) asserts that many wealthy citizens turned their *domi* (peristyle mansions) into insulae.

[8] On the patron-client system, see Moxnes 1991:244; Vanderbroeck 1987:50. On the reciprocity ethic, see Garnsey and Saller 1990:347; Macmullen 1986:521; cf. Seneca, *On Benefits*, 1.10. On mediating brokers, see Moxnes, 246; Garnsey and Saller, 348.

[9] Andrew Drummond contends that "while patron-client bonds rested ultimately on the mutual self-interest of both parties and their peers, this was overlaid with norms of mutual obligation which considerations of honor (and more general social pressures) required the patron in particular to observe, a feature also perhaps implied in the description of the *cliens* as 'in the *fides* of his patron'" (1989: 101).

[10] Robert Jewett (1986:121) asserts that although most of the inhabitants of Thessalonica were Greek, some were also Italian.

NOTES TO CONCLUSION

[1] On the problems of transparency and representation, see Roland Barthes 1975:33, 56; J. Baudrillard 1983:19.

[2] In an excellent study of the ancient Roman views of women from the second century BCE to the second century CE, Judith Hallett asserts that some Roman writers, clearly acknowledged elsewhere to be misogynists, lauded the oratorical, political and military skills of elite

women not because of the women's intrinsic abilities but because the women had blood ties with great men who were famous for the same skills (1989:59-78).

[3] While Paul uses a maternal image in 2:7, the nurse's role is that of nurturing or aiding in the maturation of children. And as we have noted, in the consolatory tradition, the model or standard for maturation is the male figure.

[4] Even the suggestion that the term "brothers" (adelphoi) refers to both men and women does not eradicate the patriarchy. On another patriarchal term, the word "man," Walter Lowe has noted, "it is disingenuous to claim that the term 'man' includes women as well, when it is used in a social setting distorted by a long history of male dominance" (1993:20).

[5] Ellingworth and Nida (1969:19) have noted the occasional transitional nature of the term adelphoi.

[6] To see the distinctive and exclusivist character of the term "brother," we may take as an example 4:9-12, where Paul applies the familial term thrice to oppose "brothers" to outsiders (tous exō). And in 4:13, Paul uses the term "brothers" in opposition to the term "the rest" (hoi loipoi). Furthermore, he opposes the "they" of 5:3 (legōsin, "they say") to "brothers" (adelphoi) in 5:4. In giving these oppositions, Paul is clearly distinguishing the believers from others.

[7] Whether Paul spoke of God as "father" as a direct and inclusive critique of the Roman government's imperial patronage theology we cannot say in this study. Yet, as Mary Rose D'Angelo notes, "apocalyptic expectations, far from being apolitical, were (as the Romans recognized) profoundly political" (1992:611-30).

[8] One reason for my reconstruction of Paul's rhetoric is my desire to find a middle ground between the simplistic "transparency of texts" advocates and the equally simplistic critics, who in their quest for the "historical" conditions of ancient texts, facilely presume that the ancient texts were like contemporary texts, that is, that all of them were textual productions, borne out of the kinds of political contestations and class struggles ingredient to the contemporary world. In either case, these extremist positions generalize and totalize the past and they fail to problematize the distance between the ancient texts and contemporary ones and between ancient writers and post (first and second) Enlightenment writers. On the two Enlightenments, see Jon Sobrino 1984:7-38.

[9] On the need to critique the Bible and other "great literature," rather than "to approve tacitly the existence of oppression in times past just because they are past," see Mary Ann Tolbert 1990:12.

[10] "Although Christianity did not invent patriarchy, feminist biblical scholars argue that it is a fact that the Bible has been and is invoked as a religious legitimator of women's oppression. Thus, feminist biblical hermeneutics takes seriously the historical-patriarchal

elements in the text" (Mark S. Medley 1989:6).

[11] Clarice J. Martin cogently calls attention to the ecclesiastical oppression which male imagery historically has supported when she asserts: "That the use of exclusive male language, imagery, and symbols has served as theological justification for the subordination of women in the church (as well as the larger society) is widely recognized. Sexual identity rather than interest or capability is often still determinative in decisions about patterns and structures of leadership" (1990:115).

[12] On the need to render ethically responsible interpretations which take into account the political consequences of one's textual readings, see Elisabeth Schüssler-Fiorenza 1988:3-17; Pamela J. Milne 1993:40.

[13] It is striking that some scholars continue to think that the reading conventions made popular by historical criticism are somehow "naturally" appropriate to the interpretation of the Bible without seeing how the conventions of historical criticism (e.g., objectivity and realism) actually are not the conventions of reading and writing and hearing reflected in Hellenistic literature. Rather, the conventions of historical criticism simply are the reading constructs deemed plausible by a *particular and now fading* age. The point is that reading constructs and conventions are always changing. For more on these matters, see Tolbert 1990:17.

[14] On how scholarly focus on an author may mask an attempt to give credence to one's own views, see Ronald Dworkin 1983:251, 258.

[15] Again, on interpretive communities, see Stanley Fish 1980.

BIBLIOGRAPHY

Achtemeier, Paul J. 1990. "Omne Verbum Sonat: The New Testament and the Oral Environment of Late Western Antiquity." *Journal of Biblical Literature* 109:3-27.

Adkins, Arthur W. H. 1963. "Friendship and Self-Sufficiency in Homer and Aristotle." *Classical Quarterly* 13:30-45.

Alexiou, Margaret. 1974. *The Ritual Lament in Greek Tradition.* Cambridge: Cambridge Univ.

Alter, Robert. 1989. *The Pleasures of Reading in an Ideological Age.* New York: Simon and Schuster.

Armstrong, Paul B. 1990. *Conflicting Readings: Variety and Validity in Interpretation.* Chapel Hill: Univ. of North Carolina.

Atkinson, J. E. 1985. "Seneca's *Consolatio ad Polybium.*" In *Aufstieg und Niedergang der römischen Welt: Geschichte und Kultur Roms im Spiegel der neueren Forschung* 32.2, ed. Wolfgang Haase. Berlin: Walter De Gruyter.

Aune, David. 1986. *The New Testament in its Literary Environment.* Philadelphia: Westminster.

Badian, E. 1992. "Thucydides on Rendering Speeches." *Athenaeum* 80:187-190.

Barclay, John M. 1993. "Conflict in Thessalonica." *Catholic Biblical Quarterly* 55:512-530.

Barr, William. 1981. *Claudian's Panegyric on the Fourth Consulate of Honorius.* Liverpool: Francis Cairns.

Barthes, Roland. 1975. *The Pleasure of the Text.* New York: Hill & Wang.

———. 1977. "The Death of the Author." In *Image, Music, Text,* ed. Roland Barthes. New York: Hill & Wang.

Bassler, Jouette. 1991. "Peace in All Ways." In *Pauline Theology, Vol. I,* ed. Jouette Bassler. Minneapolis: Fortress, 1991.

Baudrillard, J. 1983. *In the Shadow of the Silent Majorities.* New York: Semiotexte.

Bellemore, Jane. 1992. "The Dating of Seneca's *Ad Marciam De Consolatione.*" *Classical Quarterly* 42:219-34.

Best, Thomas F. 1983. "The Sociological Study of the New Testament: Promise and Peril of a New Discipline." *Scottish Journal of Theology* 36:181-94.

Betz, Hans Dieter. 1969. "On the Problem of the Religio-Historical Understanding of Apocalypticism." *Journal of Theological Studies* 6:134-156.

———. 1975. "The Literary Composition and Function of Paul's Letter to the Galatians." *New Testament Studies* 21:353-379.

Betz, Hans Dieter. 1979. *Galatians: A Commentary on Paul's Letter to the Churches in Galatia.* Hermeneia. Philadelphia: Fortress.

———. 1985. *2 Corinthians 8 and 9.* Philadelphia: Fortress.

Bitzer, Lloyd. 1968. "The Rhetorical Situation." *Philosophy and Rhetoric* 1:1-14.

Bjerkelund, Carl. 1967. *Parakalo: Form, Funktion und Sinn der Parakalo-Sätze in den paulinischen Briefen.* Oslo: Universitetsforlaget.

Blass, Friedrich Wilhelm and A. Debrunner. 1961. *A Greek Grammar of the NT and Other Early Christian Literature,* tr. Robert Funk. Chicago: Univ. of Chicago.

Bonner, Stanley F. 1966. "Lucan and the Declamation Schools." *American Journal of Philology* 87:257-289.

———. 1977. *Education in Ancient Rome: From the Elder Cato to the Younger Pliny.* Berkeley: Univ. of California.

Borg, Marcus J. 1988. "A Renaissance in Jesus Studies." *Theology Today* 45:280-292.

Bowra, C. M. 1933. "Aeneas and the Stoic Ideal." *Greece and Rome* 3: 8-21.

Bradley, K. R. 1991. *Discovering the Roman Family: Studies in Roman Social History.* New York: Oxford Univ.

Brown, Frank E. 1979. *Roman Architecture.* New York: George Braziller.

Brown, Peter. 1992. *Power and Persuasion in Late Antiquity: Towards a Christian Empire.* Madison, Wisconsin: Univ. of Wisconsin.

Bruce, F. F. 1982. *1 and 2 Thessalonians.* Waco, Texas: Word.

Bubenik, Vit. 1989. *Hellenistic and Roman Greece as a Socio-Linguistic Area.* Amsterdam: John Benjamin.

Burke, Kenneth. 1953. *Counter-Statement.* Los Altos, CA: Hermes.

———. 1969. *A Rhetoric of Motives.* Berkeley: Univ. of California.

Campbell, J. B. 1984. *The Emperor and the Roman Army: 31 BC-AD 235.* Oxford: Clarendon.

Castelli, Elizabeth A. 1991. *Imitating Paul: A Discourse of Power.* Louisville: Westminster.

Clarke, M. L. 1953. *Rhetoric at Rome: A Historical Survey.* London: Cohen and West.

Classen, Joachim. 1992. "St. Paul's Epistles and Ancient Greek and Roman Rhetoric." *Rhetorica* 10:319-344.

Clausen, Christopher. 1984. "Sherlock Holmes, Order, and the Late-Victorian Mind." *The Georgia Review* 38:104-23.

Cohen, Ralph. 1985. "History and Genre." *New Literary History* 17: 203-32.

Cooper, Lane. 1966. "An Aristotelian Analysis of 'The Gettysburg Address'." In *The Problem of Style,* ed. J. V. Cunningham. Greenwich, Connecticut: Fawcett Publications.

Cotton, Hannah. 1985. "Mirificum Genus Commendationis: Cicero and the Latin Letter of Recommendation." *American Journal of Philology* 106:328-34.

Cribiore, Raffaella. 1992. "The Happy Farmer: A Student in Composition from Roman Egypt." *Greek, Byzantine and Roman Studies* 33:247-63.

D'Angelo, Mary Rose. 1992. "*Abba* and 'Father': Imperial Theology and the Jesus Traditions." *Journal of Biblical Literature* 111:611-630.

Daitz, Stephen G. 1960. "Tacitus' Technique of Character Portrayal." *American Journal of Philology* 81:30-52.

Darr, John. 1990. *On Character Building: The Reader and the Rhetoric of Characterization in Luke-Acts.* Louisville: Westminster/John Knox.

Deissmann, Adolf. 1910. *Light from the Ancient East,* tr. Lionel Strachan. New York: Hodder and Stoughton.

DeLacy, Phillip. 1941. "Cicero's Invective Against Piso." *Transactions of the American Philological Association* 72:49-58.

—— and Benedict Einarson. 1959. *Plutarch's Moralia.* Cambridge: Harvard Univ.

Dewey, Joanna. 1980. *Markan Public Debate: Literary Techniques, Concentric Structure and Theology in Mark 2:1-3:6.* SBLDS. Missoula, MT: Scholars.

Dibelius, Martin. 1937. *An die Thessalonicher I,II; An die Philipper.* Tübingen: Mohr.

Dionisopoulos, George N., Victoria J. Gallagher, Steven R. Goldzwig and David Zarefsky. 1992. "Martin Luther King, The American Dream and Vietnam: A Collision of Rhetorical Trajectories." *Western Journal of Communication* 56:91-107.

Donelson, Lewis R. 1986. *Pseudepigraphy and Ethical Argument in the Pastoral Epistles.* Tübingen: J.C.B. Mohr-Paul Siebeck.

Donfried, Karl. 1985. "The Cults of Thessalonica and the Thessalonian Correspondence." *New Testament Studies* 31:336-47.

——. 1989. "The Theology of 1 Thessalonians as a Reflection of its Purpose." In *To Touch the Text: Biblical and Related Studies in Honor of Joseph A. Fitzmyer,* ed. Maurya Horgan and Paul Kobelski. New York: Crossroad.

Dover, K. J. 1974. *Greek Popular Morality in the Time of Plato and Aristotle.* Berkeley: Univ. of California.

Dowling, William. 1991. *The Epistolary Moment: The Poetics of the Eighteenth Century Verse Epistle.* Princeton: Princeton Univ.

Downey, Sharon. 1993. "The Evolution of the Rhetorical Genre of Apologia." *Western Journal of Communication* 57:42-64.

Droge, Arthur J. and James D. Tabor. 1992. *A Noble Death: Suicide and Martyrdom among Christians and Jews in Antiquity.* San Francisco: Harper.

Drummond, Andrew. 1989. "Early Roman Clientes." In *Patronage in Ancient Society,* ed. Andrew Wallace-Hadriel. London: Routledge.

Duff, Paul. 1991. "Metaphor, Motif and Meaning: The Rhetorical Strategy behind the Image 'Led in Triumph' in 2 Corinthians 2:14." *Catholic Biblical Quarterly* 53:79-92.

Dworkin, Ronald. 1983. "Law as Interpretation." In *The Politics of*

Interpretation, ed. W.J.T. Mitchell. Chicago: Univ. of Chicago.

Edwards, Catherine. 1993. *The Politics of Immorality in Ancient Rome*. Cambridge: Cambridge Univ.

Edwards, Douglas. 1987. "Acts of the Apostles and Chariton's *Chaereas and Callirhoe*." Ph.D. diss., Boston Univ.

———. 1989. "Acts of the Apostles and the Greco-Roman World: Narrative Communication in Social Context." In *1989 Annual SBL Seminar Papers*, ed. David Lull. Atlanta: Scholars.

Ellingworth, Paul, and Eugene Nida. 1969. *A Translator's Handbook on 1 Thessalonians*. Leiden: Brill.

Fern, Mary Edmond. 1941. *The Latin Consolatio as a Literary Type*. St Louis, Missouri: Saint Louis Univ.

Fiore, Benjamin. 1986. *The Function of Personal Example in the Socratic and Pastoral Epistles*. Rome: Biblical Institute.

Fish, Stanley. 1980. *Is There a Text in this Class?: The Authority of Interpretive Communities*. Cambridge: Harvard Univ. 1980.

———. 1989. *Doing What Comes Naturally: Change, Rhetoric, and the Practice of Theory in Literary and Legal Studies*. Durham: Duke Univ.

Fitzgerald, John T. 1988. *Cracks in an Earthen Vessel: An Examination of the Catalogues of Hardships in the Corinthian Correspondence*. Atlanta: Scholars.

Foucault, Michel. 1977. "Nietzsche, Genealogy, History." In *Language, Counter-Memory, Practice*, ed. Donald Bouchard. Ithaca, NY: Cornell Univ.

Fowler, Robert. 1991. *Let the Reader Understand: Reader Response Criticism and the Gospel of Mark*. Minneapolis: Fortress.

Freudenburg, Kirk. 1993. *The Walking Muse: Horace on the Theory of Satire*. Princeton: Princeton Univ.

Gahan, John J. 1985. "Seneca, Ovid and Exile." *The Classical World* 78:145-147.

Gamberini, Federico. 1983. *Stylistic Theory and Practice in the Younger Pliny*. New York: Olms-Weidmann.

Garnsey, Peter and Richard Saller. 1990. "Social Relations." In *From Augustus to Nero: The First Dynasty of Imperial Rome*, ed. Ronald Mellor. East Lansing, MI: Michigan.

Garrett, Susan R. 1989. *The Demise of the Devil: Magic and the Demonic in Luke's Writings*. Minneapolis: Fortress, 1989.

Geertz, Clifford. 1973. *Interpretation of Cultures*. New York: Basic Books.

Gentili, Bruno. 1988. *Poetry and its Public: From Homer to the Fifth Century*, trans. with an introduction by A. Thomas Cole. Baltimore: Johns Hopkins.

Gilliard, Frank. 1989. "The Problem of the Anti-Semitic Comma between 1 Thessalonians 2:14 and 15." *New Testament Studies* 35:481-502.

Gilmore, Michael T. 1985. *American Romanticism and the Marketplace*. Chicago: Univ. of Chicago.

Goins, Scott. 1993. "Two Aspects of Virgil's Use of Labor in the *Aeneid*." *Classical Journal* 88: 375-84.

Goldfarb, Barry. 1992. "The Conflict of Obligations in Euripides' *Alcetis*." *Greek, Roman and Byzantine Studies* 33:109-126.

Gooch, Paul W. 1987. *Partial Knowledge: Philosophical Studies in Paul.* Notre Dame: Univ. of Notre Dame.

Grant, Michael and Rachel Kitzinger. 1988. *Civilization of the Ancient Mediterranean: Greece and Rome.* ed. Michael Grant and Rachel Kitzinger. New York: Charles Scribner's Sons.

Gray, V. J. 1986. "Xenophon's *Hiero* and the Meeting of the Wise Man and Tyrant in Greek Literature." *Classical Quarterly* 36:115-123.

Gregg, Robert C. 1975. *Consolation Philosophy: Greek and Christian Paideia in Basil And the Two Gregories.* Cambridge: The Philadelphia Patristic Foundation, Ltd.

Grotius, Hugo. 1679. *Opera Omnia Theologica.* Amsterdam: Blaev.

Grundy, Robert. 1987. "The Hellenization of Dominical Tradition and Christianization of Jewish Tradition in the Eschatology of 1-2 Thessalonians." *New Testament Studies* 33:161-178.

Habinik, Thomas. 1992. "An Aristocracy of Virtue: Seneca on the Beginnings of Wisdom." *Yale Classical Studies* 29 (1992):187-203.

Hadas, Moses. 1958. *The Stoic Philosophy of Seneca: Essays and Letters of Seneca.* Garden City, NY: Doubleday.

Hagner, Donald A. 1993. "Paul's Quarrel with Judaism." In *Anti-Semitism and Christianity: Issues of Polemic and Faith.* Minneapolis: Fortress.

Hahn, Paul Douglas. 1990. "Structure in Rhetorical Criticism and the Structure of the Sermon on the Plain (Luke 6:20-49)." Ph.D. diss., Marquette Univ.

Hall, Robert. 1987. "The Rhetorical Outline for Galatians: A Reconsideration." *Journal of Biblical Literature* 106:277-87.

———. 1991. "Historical Influence and Rhetorical Effect: Another Look at Galatians 1 and 2." *Persuasive Artistry: Studies in New Testament in Honor of George A. Kennedy,* ed., Duane F. Watson. Sheffield: *Journal for the Study Of the Old Testament.*

Hallett, Judith. 1989. "Women as Same and Other in the Classical Roman Elite." *Helios* 16:59-78.

Halliwell, Stephen. 1990. "Traditional Greek Conceptions of Characters." In *Characterization and Individuality in Greek Literature,* ed. C. B. R. Pelling. Oxford: Clarendon.

Hariman, Robert. 1992. "Decorum, Power and the Courtly Style." *Quarterly Journal of Speech* 78:149-172.

Harris, Trudier. 1991. *Fiction and Folklore: The Novels of Toni Morrison.* Knoxville: Univ. of Tennessee.

Hart, P. Roderick. 1986. "Contemporary Scholarship in Public Address." *Western Journal of Communication* 50:283-295.

Hendrix, Holland. 1984. "Thessalonians Honor Romans." Ph.D. diss., Harvard Univ.

Hendrix, Holland. 1986. "Beyond 'Imperial Cult' and 'Cults of Magistrates'." In *1986 SBL Seminar Papers*, ed. Kent Harold Richards. Atlanta: Scholars.

———. 1991. "Archaeology and Eschatology at Thessalonica." In *The Future of Early Christianity: Essays in Honor of Helmut Koester*, ed. Birger A. Pearson. Minneapolis: Fortress.

Hewitt, Joseph William. 1927. "The Terminology of 'Gratitude' in Greek." *Classical Philology* 22:142-161.

Highet, Gilbert. 1976. *The Classical Tradition: Greek and Roman Influences on Western Literature*. New York: Oxford Univ.

Hijmans, B. L., Jr. 1976. *Inlaboratus et Facilis: Aspects of Structure in Some Letters of Seneca*. Leiden, Netherlands: E. J. Brill.

Hock, Ronald. 1980. *The Social Context of Paul's Ministry: Tentmaking and Apostleship*. Philadelphia: Fortress.

———. 1988. "The Greek Novel." In *Greco-Roman Literature and the New Testament*, ed. David E. Aune. Atlanta: Scholars.

——— and Edward O'Neil. 1986. *The Chreia in Ancient Rhetoric, Vol. I: The Progymnasmata*. Atlanta: Scholars.

Hodgson, Robert, Jr. 1986. "Holiness Tradition and Social Description: Intertestamental Judaism and Early Christianity." In *Reading Beyond Chapters in the History of Perfectionism*, ed. Stanley M. Burgess. Peabody, MA: Hendrickson Publishers.

Holmberg, Bengt. 1990. *Sociology and the New Testament: An Appraisal*. Minneapolis: Fortress.

Hutcheon, Linda. 1988. *A Poetics of Postmodernism*. New York: Routledge.

Iser, Wolfgang. 1974. *The Act of Reading: A Theory of Aesthetic Response*. Baltimore: Johns Hopkins Univ.

Jauss, Hans. 1982. "Literary History as a Challenge to Literary Theory." In *Toward an Aesthetics of Reception*, trans. Timothy Bahti. Minneapolis: Univ. of Minnesota.

Jeremias, Joachim. 1958. "Chiasmus in den Paulusbriefen." *Zeitschrift für die neutestamentliche Wissenschaft* 49:145-56.

Jewett, Robert. 1979. *Jesus Against the Rapture: Seven Unexpected Prophecies*. Philadelphia: Westminster.

———. 1986. *The Thessalonian Correspondence: Pauline Rhetoric and Millenarian Piety*. Philadelphia: Fortress.

Johanson, Bruce C. 1987. *To All the Brethren: A Text-Linguistic and Rhetorical Approach to I Thessalonians*. Stockholm: Almqvist & Wiksell International.

Johnson, Luke T. 1986. *The Writings of the New Testament: An Interpretation*. Philadelphia: Fortress.

———. 1989. "The New Testament's Anti-Jewish Slander and the Conventions of Ancient Polemic." *Journal of Biblical Literature* 108: 419-41.

Jones, A. H. M. 1964. "The Hellenistic Age." *Past and Present* 27:3-22.

Kaemmel, Ernest. 1983. "Literature under the Table: The Detective Novel and its Social Mission." In *The Poetics of Murder: Detective Fiction and Literary Theory*, ed. Glenn W. Most and William W. Stowe. San Diego: Harcourt Brace Jovanovich.

Keck, Leander E. and Victor Paul Furnish. 1984. *The Pauline Letters*. Nashville: Abingdon.

Keitel, Elizabeth. 1984. "Principate and Civil War in the *Annals of Tacitus*." *American Journal of Philology* 105:306-25.

Kennedy, George. 1968. "The Rhetoric of Advocacy in Greece and Rome." *American Journal of Philology* 89:419-36.

———. 1969. *Quintilian*. New York: Twayne.

———. 1984. *New Testament Interpretation Through Rhetorical Criticism*. Chapel Hill: Univ. of North Carolina.

Kimberling, Ronald C. 1982. *Kenneth Burke's Dramatism and Popular Arts*. Bowling Green, Kentucky: Bowling Green State Univ.

Kinneavy, James L. 1986. *"Kairos: A Neglected Concept."* In *Rhetoric and Praxis: The Contribution of Classical Rhetoric to Practical Reasoning*, ed. Jean Dietz Moss. Washington, DC: Catholic Univ. of America.

Kirby, John T. 1990. *The Rhetoric of Cicero's Pro Cluentio*. Amsterdam: J. C. Gieben.

Kloppenborg, John S. 1993. *"Philadelphia, Theodidaktos* and the Dioscuri: Rhetorical Engagement in 1 Thessalonians 4:9-12." *New Testament Studies* 39:265-289.

Koester, Helmut. 1979. "1 Thessalonians—Experiment in Christian Writing." In *Continuity and Discontinuity in Church History*, ed. F. Forrester Church and T. George. Leiden: Brill.

———. 1982. *Introduction to the New Testament, Vol. I: History, Culture and Religion of the Hellenistic Age*. Philadelphia: Fortress.

———. 1992. "Jesus the Victim." *Journal of Biblical Literature* 111:3-15.

Koskenniemi, Heikki. 1956. *Studien zur Idee und Phraseologie des griechischen Briefes bis 400 n. Chr.* Helsinki: Akateeminen Kirjakauppa.

Kuck, David. 1992. *Judgment and Community: Paul's Use of Apocalyptic Judgment Language in 1 Corinthians 3:5-4:5*. Leiden: E. J. Brill.

Lawall, Gilbert. 1958. "Exempla and Theme in Juvenal's Tenth Satire." *Transactions of the American Philological Association* 89:25-31.

Lock, Helen Mary. 1991. "A Case of Mis-taken Identity: Detective Undercurrents in Recent African-American Fiction." Ph.D. diss., Univ. of Virginia.

Long, A. A. 1986. *Hellenistic Philosophy: Stoics, Epicureans, Sceptics*. Berkeley: Univ. of California.

Longino, Helen E. 1990. *Science as Social Knowledge: Values and Objectivity in Scientific Inquiry*. Princeton: Princeton Univ.

Lowe, Walter. 1993. *Theology and Difference: The Wound of Reason*. Bloomington, IN: Indiana Univ.

Lüdemann, Gerd. 1984. *Paul, Apostle to the Gentiles: Studies in Chro-*

nology, tr. F. Stanley Jones with a foreword by John Knox. Philadelphia: Fortress.

Lyons, George. 1985. *Pauline Autobiography: Towards a New Understanding*. SBLDS 73. Atlanta: Scholars.

Mack, Burton. 1990. *Rhetoric and the New Testament*. Minneapolis: Fortress.

Macmullen, Ramsay. 1986. "Personal Power in the Roman Empire." *American Journal of Philology* 107:512-24.

Malherbe, Abraham. 1970. "Gentle as a Nurse: The Cynic Background to 1 Thess 2." *Novum Testamentum* 12:203-17.

——. 1972. "1 Thessalonians as a Paraenetic Letter." A Paper presented to the SBL Seminar on Paul in Los Angeles, CA.

——. 1983. "Exhortation in First Thessalonians." *Novum Testamentum* 25:238-56.

——. 1985. "'Not in a Corner': Early Christian Apologetic in Acts 26:26." *Second Century* 5:193-210.

——. 1986. *Moral Exhortation: A Greco-Roman Sourcebook*. Philadelphia: Westminster.

——. 1987. *Paul and the Thessalonians: The Philosophic Tradition of Pastoral Care*. Philadelphia: Fortress.

——. 1989. *Paul and the Popular Philosophers*. Minnesota: Fortress.

——. 1990. "'Pastoral Care' in the Thessalonian Church." *New Testament Studies* 36:375-391.

Manning, C. E. 1981. *On Seneca's "Ad Marciam."* Leiden: E. J. Brill.

Marshall, Peter. 1987. *Enmity in Corinth: Social Conventions in Paul's Relations with the Corinthians*. Tübingen: J. C. B. Mohr.

Martin, Clarice J. 1990. "Inclusive Language and the Brief Statement of Faith: Widening the Margins in Our Common Confession. In *To Confess the Faith Today*, ed. Jack L. Stotts and Jane Dempsey Douglas. Louisville: Westminster/John Knox.

Martin, Dale. 1990. *Slavery as Salvation: The Metaphor of Slavery in Pauline Christianity*. New Haven: Yale.

Martin, Herbert and Jane E. Phillips. 1978. "*Consolatio Ad Uxorem* Moralia 608A-612B." In *Plutarch's Ethical Writings and Early Christian Literature*, ed. Hans Dieter Betz. Leiden: Brill.

Martindale, Charles. 1991. "Redeeming the Text: The Validity of Comparisons of Classical and Postclassical Literature (A View from Britain)." *Arion* 1:45-75.

Mason, John Philip. 1989. "Paul's Understanding of the Resurrection in 1 Thessalonians 4:13-18." Ph.D. diss., Southern Baptist Theological Seminary.

Mason, Theodore O. 1988. "The Novelist and Conservator: Stories and Comprehension in Toni Morrison's *Song of Solomon*." *Contemporary Literature* 29:564-81.

May, James M. 1981. *Trials of Character: The Eloquence of Ciceronian Ethos*. Chapel Hill: Univ. of North Carolina, 1981.

Mbalia, Doreatha Drummond. 1991. *Toni Morrison's Developing Class Consciousness.* Selinsgrove: Susquehanna Univ.

McGushin, P. 1964. "Virgil and the Spirit of Endurance." *American Journal of Philology* 85:225-253.

McKay, A. G. 1975. *Houses, Villas and Palaces in the Roman World.* Ithaca: Cornell Univ.

McKnight, Scot. 1993. "A Loyal Critic: Matthew's Polemic with Judaism in Theological Perspective." In *Anti-Semitism and Early Christianity: Issues of Polemic and Faith,* ed. Craig A. Evans and Donald A. Hagner. Minneapolis: Fortress.

Medley, Mark S. 1989. "Emancipatory Solidarity: the Redemptive Significance of Jesus in Mark." *Perspectives in Religious Studies* 21:5-22.

Meeks, Wayne. 1983. *The First Urban Christians: The Social World of the Apostle Paul.* New Haven: Yale Univ.

———. 1986. *The Moral World of the First Christians.* Philadelphia: Westminster.

———. 1990. "The Circle of Reference in Pauline Morality." In *Greeks, Romans, and Christians: Essays in Honor of Abraham J. Malherbe,* ed. David L. Balch, Everett Ferguson and Wayne A. Meeks. Minneapolis: Fortress.

Meyer, Elizabeth A. 1990. "Explaining the Epigraphic Habit in the Roman Empire: The Evidence of Epitaphs." *Journal of Roman Studies* 80:74-96.

Miller, Arthur. 1972. "Rhetorical Exigence." *Philosophy and Rhetoric* 5: 111-118.

Miller, Carolyn. 1984. "Genre as Social Action." *Quarterly Journal of Speech* 70:151-67.

Milne, Pamela J. 1993. "What Shall We Do with Judith?: A Feminist Reassessment of a Biblical 'Heroine'." *Semeia* 62:37-58.

Mitchell, Alan. 1992. "The Social Function of Friendship in Acts 2:44-47 and 4:32-37." *Journal of Biblical Literature* 111:255-272.

Mitchell, Margaret. 1989. "Paul and the Rhetoric of Reconciliation: An Exegetical Investigation of the Language and Composition of 1 Corinthians." Ph.D. diss., Univ. of Chicago. [Published in 1992 under the same title by Westminster/John Knox, Louisville, KY.]

———. 1989a. "Concerning *peri de* in 1 Corinthians." *Novum Testamentum* 31:229-256.

Morford, Mark P. O. 1992. "*Iubes Esse Liberos*: Pliny's *Panegyricus* and Liberty." *American Journal of Philology* 113:575-593.

Morrison, Toni. 1977. *Song of Solomon.* New York: Penguin.

———. 1984. "Memory, Creation, and Writing." *Thought* 59:385-90.

———. 1987. *Beloved: A Novel.* New York: Knopf.

Morrow, Stanley. 1982. "*Parresia* in the New Testament." *Catholic Biblical Quarterly* 44:431-446.

Moskalew, Walter. 1982. *Formular Language and Poetic Design.* Leiden: E.J. Brill.

Most, Glenn W. 1989. "The Stranger's Strategem: Self-Disclosure and Self-Sufficiency in Greek Culture." *Journal of Hellenic Studies* 109:114-33.

Moxnes, Halvor. 1991. "Patron-Client Relations and the New Community in Luke-Acts." In *The Social World of Luke-Acts. Models for Interpretation*, ed. Jerome Neyrey. Peabody, MA: Hendrickson.

Muilenburg, James. 1969. "Form Criticism and Beyond." *Journal of Biblical Literature* 88:1-18.

Murphy, James. 1990. "A Time of Shame and Sorrow: Robert F. Kennedy and the American Jeremiad." *Quarterly Journal of Speech* 76:401-414.

Murray, Gilbert. 1955. *The Five Stages of Greek Religion*. Garden City, NY: Doubleday and Co.

Nagle, Betty Rose. 1980. *The Poetics of Exile: Program and Polemic in the Tristia and Epistulae ex Ponto of Ovid*. Bruxelles: Latomus.

Newman, Robert J. 1988. "*In Umbra Virtutis: Gloria* in the Thought of Seneca the Philosopher." *Eranos* 86:145-159.

Nicolet, Claude. 1991. *Space, Geography, and Politics in the Early Roman Empire*. Ann Arbor, MI: Univ. of Michigan.

Nock, A. D. 1941. "A Cabiric Rite." *American Journal of Archaeology* 45:577-581.

North, Helen. 1979. *From Myth to Icon: Reflections of Greek Ethical Doctrine in Literature and Art*. Ithaca, NY: Cornell.

Notopoulos, James A. 1951. "Continuity and Interconnexion in Homeric Oral Composition." *Transactions of the American Philological Association* 82:81-101.

Nutton, V. 1978. "The Beneficial Ideology." In *Imperialism in the Ancient World*, ed. P. D. Garnsey and C. R. Whittaker. Cambridge: Cambridge Univ.

O'Banion, John D. 1985. "Narration and Argumentation: Quintilian on *Narratio* as the Heart of Rhetorical Thinking." *Rhetorica* 3:325-351.

Ober, Josiah. 1989. *Mass and Elite in Democratic Athens: Rhetoric, Ideology, and the Power of the People*. Princeton: Princeton Univ.

Parunak, H. Van Dyke. 1981. "Oral Typesetting: Some Uses of Biblical Structure." *Biblica* 62:153-168.

———. 1983. "Transitional Techniques in the Bible." *Journal of Biblical Literature* 102:525-548.

Patte, Daniel. 1983. *Paul's Faith and the Power of the Gospel*. Philadelphia: Fortress.

Perelman, Chaim. 1979. *The New Rhetoric and the Humanities: Essays on Rhetoric and its Application*, tr. William Kluback. Dordrecht: D. Reidel.

Perkins, Pheme. 1989. "1 Thessalonians and Hellenistic Religious Practices." In *To Touch the Text: Biblical and Related Studies in Honor of Joseph A. Fitzmyer*, ed. Maurya Horgan and Paul Kobelski. New York: Crossroad.

Pfitzner, Victor. 1967. *Paul and the Agon Motif*. Leiden: E.J. Brill.

Porter, David H. 1971. "Structural Parallelism in Greek Tragedy: A

Preliminary Study." *Transactions of the American Philological Association* 102:465-496.

Post, L. A. 1960. "Virtue Promoted in Menander's *Dyskolos.*" *Transactions of the American Philological Association* 91:152-161.

Poulakos, Takis. 1990. "Historiographics of the Tradition of Rhetoric: A Brief History of Classical Funeral Orations." *Western Journal of Communication* 34:172-188.

Rabinowitz, Peter. 1977. "Truth in Fiction: A Reexamination of Audience." *Critical Inquiry* 4:121-141.

———. 1987. *Before Reading: Narrative Conventions and the Politics of Interpretation.* Ithaca: Cornell Univ.

Railton, Stephen. 1991. *Authorship and Audience: Literary Performance in the American Renaissance.* Princeton, NJ: Princeton.

Ramage, Edwin S. 1960. "Early Roman Urbanity." *American Journal of Philology* 81:65-72.

———. 1966. "City and Country in Menander's 'Dyskolos'." *Philologus* 110:194-211.

———. 1987. *The Nature and Purpose of Augustus' "Res Gestae."* Stutgart: Franz Steiner.

Richard, Earl. 1991. "Contemporary Research on 1 (and 2) Thessalonians." *Biblical Theology Bulletin* 20:107-115.

Riesenberg, Peter. 1992. *Citizenship in the Western Tradition: Plato to Rousseau.* Chapel Hill: Univ. of North Carolina.

Robbins, Vernon. 1988. "The Chreia." In *Greco-Roman Literature and the New Testament,* ed. David Aune. Atlanta: Scholars.

Roetzel, Calvin. 1972. "1 Thessalonians 5:12-28: A Case Study." In *Society of Biblical Literature Seminar Papers,* ed. Lane McGaughy. Chico: Society of Biblical Literature.

Rogers, G. M. 1991. "Demosthenes of Oneonda and Models of *Euergetism.*" *Journal of Roman Studies* 81:91-100.

Romm, James S. 1992. *The Edges of the Earth in Ancient Thought: Geography, Exploration, and Fiction.* Princeton: Princeton Univ.

Russell, D. A. 1973. *Plutarch.* New York: Charles Scribner's Sons.

Ryan, Eugene. 1984. *Aristotle's Theory of Rhetorical Argumentation.* Saint-Laurent and Montreal: Les Éditions Bellarmin.

Saller, Richard P. 1982. *Personal Patronage Under the Early Empire.* Cambridge: Cambridge Univ.

———. 1989. "Patronage and Friendship in Early Imperial Rome: Drawing the Distinction." In *Patronage in Ancient Society,* ed. Andrew Wallace-Hadriel. London: Routledge.

Sampley, J. Paul. 1985. "Romans and Galatians: Comparison and Contrast." In *Understanding the Word: Essays in Honor of Bernhard W. Anderson,* ed. J. T. Butler, W. Conrad, and E. C. Ollenburger. Sheffield: JSOT.

———. 1991. *Walking Between the Times.* Minneapolis: Fortress.

Sanders, Boykin. 1981. "Imitating Paul: I Cor. 4:16." *Harvard Theological Review* 74:353-363.

Schell, John Frederick. 1977. "Decorum and Shelley." Ph.D. diss., Vanderbilt Univ.

Schubert, Paul. 1939. *Form and Function of the Pauline Thanksgivings*. Berlin: Alfred Töpelmann.

Schüssler Fiorenza, Elisabeth. 1988. "The Ethics of Biblical Interpretation: Decentering Biblical Scholarship." *Journal of Biblical Literature* 107:3-17.

Scourfield, J. H. D. 1993. *Heliodorus: A Commentary on Jerome, Letter 60*. Oxford: Clarendon.

Scroggs, Robin. 1980. "The Sociological Interpretation of the N.T.: The Present State of Research." *New Testament Studies* 26:164-179.

Seckler, Josephine Evetts. 1982. "Consolatory Literature of the English Recusants." *Renaissance and Reformation* 6:122-141.

Sherk, Robert K. 1969. *Roman Documents from the Greek East: Senatus Consulta and Epistulae to the Age of Augustus*. Baltimore: Johns Hopkins.

Smit, Joop. 1989. "The Letter of Paul to the Galatians: A Deliberative Speech." *New Testament Studies* 35:1-26.

Smith, Abraham. 1989. "The Social and Ethical Implications of the Pauline Rhetoric in 1 Thessalonians." Ph.D. diss., Vanderbilt Univ.

Smith, Craig R. 1992. "Roman Decorum as a New Existential Community." *Western Journal of Communication* 56:68-89.

——. and Michael J. Hyde. 1991. "Rethinking 'the Public': The Role of Emotion in Being-With Others." *Quarterly Journal of Speech* 77:446-466.

Sobrino, Jon. 1984. *The True Church and the Poor*, trans. Matthew J. O'Connell. Maryknoll, NY: Orbis.

Solomon, Martha. 1993. "Covenanted Rights: The Metaphoric Matrix of 'I Have a Dream.'" In *Martin Luther King, Jr., and the Sermonic Power of Public Discourse*, ed. Carolyn Calloway-Thomas and John Louis Lucaites. Tuscaloosa, AL: Univ. of Alabama.

Sourvinou-Inwood, Christiane. 1989. "Assumptions and the Creation of Meaning: Reading Sophocles' *Antigone*." *Journal of Hellenic Studies* 109:134-148.

Spencer, Aida. 1984. *Paul's Literary Style*. Jackson, MS: Evangelical Theological Society.

Stadter, Philip A. 1987. "The Rhetoric of Plutarch's Pericles." *Ancient Society* 18:251-269.

Staehlin, Gustav. 1968. "*parakaleo*." *Theological Dictionary of the New Testament*, ed. Gerhard Kittel. Grand Rapids, MI: Eerdmans.

Stendahl, Krister. 1976. *Paul Among Jews and Gentiles and Other Essays*. Philadelphia: Fortress.

Stowers, Stanley. 1986. *Letter-Writing in Greco-Roman Antiquity*. Philadelphia: Fortress.

———. 1988. "Social Typification and Classification of Ancient Letters." In *The Social World of Formative Christianity and Judaism: Essays in Tribute to Howard Clark Kee*, ed. Jacob Neusner. Philadelphia: Fortress.

Stowers, Stanley. 1990. "Paul on the Use and Abuse of Reason." In *Greeks, Romans, and Christians: Essays in Honor of Abraham J. Malherbe*, ed. David L. Balch, Everett Ferguson and Wayne A. Meeks. Minneapolis: Fortress.

———. 1991. "Friends and Enemies in the Politics of Heaven: Reading Theology in Philippians." In *Pauline Theology, Vol. I*, ed. Jouette Bassler. Minneapolis: Fortress.

Symons, Julian. 1985. *Bloody Murder: From the Detective Novel to the Crime Novel: A History.* New York: Viking.

Theissen, Gerd. 1972. *Social Reality and the Early Christians: Theology, Ethics and the World of the New Testament*, ed. Margaret Kohl. Minneapolis: Fortress.

Tiede, David. 1980. *Prophecy and History in Luke-Acts.* Philadelphia: Fortress.

Tietze, Victoria Larson. 1985. "The Imagery of Morality in Seneca's Prose-Works." Ph.D. diss., McMaster Univ.

———. 1992. "Seneca and the Schools of Philosophy in Early Imperial Rome." *Illinois Classical Studies* 17:49-56.

Tolbert, Mary Ann. 1989. *Sowing the Gospel: Mark's World in Literary-Historical Perspective.* Philadelphia: Fortress.

———. 1990. "Protestant Feminists and the Bible: On the Horns of a Dilemma." In *The Pleasure of Her Text: Feminist Readings of Biblical and Historical Texts*, ed. Alice Bach. Philadelphia: Trinity Press International.

Toynbee, J. M. C. 1944. "Dictators and Philosophers in the First Century A.D." *Greece and Rome* 13:43-58.

Vanderbroeck, Paul. 1987. *Popular Leadership and Collective Behavior in the Late Roman Republic (ca 80-50 BC).* Amsterdam: J. C. Gieben.

Vasaly, Ann. 1985. "The Masks of Rhetoric: Cicero's *Pro Roscio Amerina.*" *Rhetorica* 3:1-20.

———. 1993. *Representations: Images of the World in Ciceronian Oratory.* Berkeley: Univ. of California.

Vatz, Richard. 1973. "The Myth of the Rhetorical Situation." *Philosophy and Rhetoric* 6:154-61.

Vickers, M. 1976. "Thessalonike." *The Princeton Encyclopedia of Classical Sites*, ed. Richard Stillwell. Princeton: Princeton.

Volf, Judith M. Gundry. 1990. *Paul and Perseverance: Staying In and Falling Away.* Louisville: Westminster/John Knox.

Wardman, Alan. 1974. *Plutarch's Lives.* Berkeley: Univ. of California.

Watson, Duane F. 1988. "A Rhetorical Analysis of Philippians and its Implications for the Unity Question." *Novum Testamentum* 30:57-88.

———. 1989. "1 Corinthians 10:23-11:1 in the Light of Greco-Roman

Rhetoric: The Role of Rhetorical Questions." *Journal of Biblical Literature* 108:301-318.

Watson, Duane F. 1993. "James 2 in Light of Greco-Roman Schemes of Argumentation." *New Testament Studies* 39:94-121.

Weatherly, Jon A. 1991. "The Authenticity of 1 Thessalonians 2:13-16: Additional Evidence." *Journal for the Study of the New Testament* 42:79-98.

Weinrib, Ernst Joseph. 1990. *The Spaniards in Rome: from Marinus to Domitian.* New York: Garland.

Welch, John W. 1981. *Chiasmus in Antiquity: Structures, Analyses, Exegesis.* Gerstenberg: Hildesheim.

Whitaker, Richard. 1983. *Myth and Personal Experience in Roman Love-Elegy: A Study in Poetic Technique.* Göttingen: Vandenhoeck and Ruprecht.

White, Leland J. 1986. "Grid and Group in Matthew's Community: The Righteousness/Honor Code in the Sermon on the Mount." *Semeia* 35:61-90.

White, John L. 1986. *Light from Ancient Letters.* Philadelphia: Fortress.

Wiles, G. P. 1974. *Paul's Intercessory Prayers: The Significance of the Intercessory Prayer Passages in the Letters of St. Paul.* Cambridge: Cambridge Univ.

Wills, Garry. 1992. *Lincoln at Gettysburg: The Words that Remade America.* New York: Simon & Schuster.

Wilson, John R. 1989. "Shifting and Permanent *Philia* in Thucydides." *Greece and Rome* 36:147-151.

Woodman, Tony and Jonathan Powell. 1992. "Epilogue." In *Author and Audience in Latin Literature,* ed. Tony Woodman and Jonathan Powell. Cambridge: Cambridge Univ.

Wuellner, Wilhelm. 1986. "The Argumentative Structure of 1 Thessalonians as Paradoxical Encomium." A revised edition of a paper presented to the SBL Seminar on Paul in Atlanta, GA.

Yarbrough, O. Larry. 1985. *Not Like the Gentiles: Marriage Rules in the Letters of Paul.* Atlanta: Scholars.

Ziolkowski, John. 1981. *Thucydides and the Tradition of Funeral Speeches at Athens.* New York: Arno.

INDEXES

AUTHORS

Achtemeier, Paul J. 30
Adkins, Arthur W. H 119
Alexiou, Margaret 47
Alter, Robert 17, 20, 31, 110
Armstrong, Paul B. 19-21, 110
Atkinson, J. E. 52, 65, 122, 123
Aune, David 129
Badian, E. 113
Barclay, John M. 61, 119
Barr, William 121
Barthes, Roland 105, 137
Bassler, Jouette 73, 74
Baudrillard, J. 137
Bellemore, Jane 125
Best, Thomas F. 21
Betz, Hans Dieter 120, 125, 133
Bitzer, Lloyd 111, 128
Bjerkelund, Carl 47
Blass, Friedrich Wilhelm 135
Bonner, Stanley F. 34, 135
Borg, Marcus J. 13
Bowra, C. M. 126
Bradley, K. R. 118, 133
Brown, Frank E. 137
Brown, Peter 29
Bruce, F. F. 82, 121, 131, 134
Bubenik, Vit 28
Burke, Kenneth 43, 120
Campbell, J. B. 112
Castelli, Elizabeth A. 20
Clarke, M. L. 28
Classen, Joachim 113, 130
Clausen, Christopher 42, 120
Cohen, Ralph 120
Cooper, Lane 111
Cotton, Hannah 45
Cribiore, Raffaella 37
D'Angelo, Mary Rose 74, 138
Daitz, Stephen G. 34
Darr, John 35

Debrunner, A. 135
Deissmann, Adolf 82
DeLacy, Phillip 34, 50
Dewey, Joanna 69, 78, 131
Dibelius, Martin 134
Dionisopoulos, George N. 136
Donelson, Lewis R. 31, 115
Donfried, Karl 99, 123
Dover, K. J. 47
Dowling, William 129
Downey, Sharon 42
Droge, Arthur J. 123
Drummond, Andrew 137
Duff, Paul 56, 126
Dworkin, Ronald 139
Edwards, Catherine 33, 115
Edwards, Douglas 18, 28
Einarson, Benedict 50, 122
Ellingworth, Paul 131, 133, 138
Fern, Mary Edmond 50, 52, 58,
    122, 124, 130, 132, 133
Fiore, Benjamin 31, 113-116
Fish, Stanley 110, 139
Fitzgerald, John T. 27, 56
Foucault, Michel 105
Fowler, Robert 18
Freudenburg, Kirk 114
Furnish, Victor Paul 110
Gahan, John J. 58
Gallagher, Victoria J. 136
Gamberini, Federico 30
Garnsey, Peter 137
Garrett, Susan R. 27
Geertz, Clifford 66
Gentili, Bruno 46
Gilliard, Frank 118
Gilmore, Michael T. 111
Goins, Scott 119, 126
Goldfarb, Barry 63
Goldzwig, Steven R. 136

Gooch, Paul 135
Grant, Michael 120
Gray, V. J. 35
Gregg, Robert C. 48, 50, 51, 65, 122-124, 127, 130
Grotius, Hugo 16
Grundy, Robert 88
Habinik, Thomas 116
Hadas, Moses 48
Hagner, Donald A. 35, 118
Hahn, Paul Douglas 113
Hall, Robert 34, 116, 120
Hallett, Judith 137
Halliwell, Stephen 116
Hariman, Robert 45
Harris, Trudier 61
Hart, P. Roderick 42
Hendrix, Holland 96, 98, 132
Hewitt, Joseph William 73
Highet, Gilbert 115
Hijmans, B. L., Jr. 30
Hock, Ronald 33, 38, 40, 119, 127
Hodgson, Robert, Jr. 114
Holmberg, Bengt 137
Hutcheon, Linda 120
Hyde, Michael J. 44
Iser, Wolfgang 24, 110
Jauss, Hans 24, 110
Jeremias, Joachim 30
Jewett, Robert 13, 14, 16, 19, 21, 22, 26, 46, 94, 95, 98, 99, 109, 110, 119, 121, 130, 131, 134, 136, 137
Johanson, Bruce C. 53, 121, 131, 134
Johnson, Luke T. 20, 31, 117
Jones, A. H. M. 27, 28, 48
Kaemmel, Ernest 120
Keck, Leander E. 110
Keitel, Elizabeth 33
Kennedy, George 33, 91, 112, 113, 120, 121, 130, 131, 136
Kimberling, Ronald C. 43
Kinneavy, James L. 44
King, Martin Luther, Jr. 93, 100
Kirby, John T. 15, 35, 113
Kitzenger, Rachel 120

Kloppenborg, John 27, 63, 135
Koester, Helmut 16, 97, 113
Koskenniemi, Heikki 121
Kuck, David 125
Lawall, Gilbert 32
Lock, Helen Mary 42, 120, 128
Long, A. A. 131
Longino, Helen E. 18
Lowe, Walter 138
Lüdemann, Gerd 88
Lyons, George 77, 121, 133
Mack, Burton 14, 112, 120
Macmullen, Ramsay 137
Malherbe, Abraham 13, 14, 18, 21, 22, 32, 35, 37, 40, 46, 47, 51, 53, 58, 78, 95, 96, 99, 110, 111, 118, 119, 121, 123, 124, 125, 132, 134-136
Manning, C. E. 50, 53, 58, 64, 65, 80, 122, 127, 131, 132
Marshall, Peter 35, 37
Martin, Clarice J. 139
Martin, Dale 97
Martin, Herbert 48, 50, 51, 54, 55, 123, 125, 126, 127, 128
Martindale, Charles 17, 20
Mason, John Philip 135
Mason, Theodore O. 61
May, James M. 32-33
Mbalia, Doreatha Drummond 61
McGushin, P. 126
McKay, A. G. 137
McKnight, Scot 117
Medley, Mark S. 138
Meeks, Wayne 13, 18, 21, 22, 27, 28, 45, 53, 66, 94, 95, 98, 110, 112, 137
Meyer, Elizabeth A. 98
Miller, Arthur 128
Miller, Carolyn 43
Milne, Pamela J. 139
Mitchell, Alan 129, 136
Mitchell, Margaret 31, 47, 114, 120, 121, 135
Morford, Mark P. O. 30
Morrison, Toni 61, 92, 128
Morrow, Stanley 18
Moskalew, Walter 69, 114, 131

Most, Glenn W. 119
Moxnes, Halvor 137
Muilenburg, James 69
Murphy, James 136
Murray, Gilbert 48
Nagle, Betty Rose 54, 63, 124
Newman, Robert J. 38, 87, 120, 132
Nicolet, Claude 112
Nida, Eugene 131, 133, 138
Nock, A. D. 119
North, Helen 32, 33, 116
Notopoulos, James A. 30
Nutton, V. 136
O'Banion, John D. 29
Ober, Josiah 22
O'Neil, Edward 22
Parunak, H. Van Dyke 29, 30, 68, 131
Patte, Daniel 133
Perelman, Chaim 22
Perkins, Pheme 63, 130
Pfitzner, Victor 78
Phillips, Jane E. 48, 50, 51, 54, 55, 123, 125-128
Porter, David H. 114
Post, L. A. 37, 138
Poulakos, Takis 18, 123
Powell, Jonathan 17, 18, 110-11
Rabinowitz, Peter 109, 110
Railton, Stephen 25, 111
Ramage, Edwin S. 37, 112
Richard, Earl 16
Riesenberg, Peter 112
Robbins, Vernon 115
Roetzel, Calvin 114
Rogers, G. M. 97
Romm, James S. 112
Russell, D. A. 29, 129
Ryan, Eugene 32
Saller, Richard P. 36, 63, 79, 97, 116, 137
Sampley, J. Paul 23, 45, 114, 127, 135
Sanders, Boykin 132
Schell, John Frederick 45
Schubert, Paul 47
Schüssler Fiorenza, Elisabeth 139

Scourfield, J. H. D. 51, 124
Scroggs, Robin 21
Seckler, Josephine Evetts 122
Sherk, Robert K. 136
Smit, Joop 120
Smith, Abraham 22
Smith, Craig R. 44, 45, 66
Sobrino, Jon 138
Solomon, Martha 136
Sourvinou-Inwood, Christiane 19
Spencer, Aida 113
Stadter, Philip A. 121
Staehlin, Gustav 121, 122
Stendahl, Krister 20, 110
Stowers, Stanley 26, 30, 33, 43, 45, 47, 50-53, 57, 63, 85, 116, 117, 121-125, 127
Symons, Julian 42
Tabor, James D. 123
Theissen, Gerd 64
Tiede, David 112
Tietze, Victoria Larson 58, 116, 127
Tolbert, Mary Ann 28, 30, 44, 105, 111, 138, 139
Toynbee, J. M. C. 35
Vanderbroeck, Paul 137
Vasaly, Ann 35, 37, 116-17, 119
Vatz, Richard 111, 128
Vickers, M. 137
Volf, Judith M. Gundry 133
Wardman, Alan 40
Watson, Duane F. 114, 115, 120
Weatherly, Jon A. 35
Weinrib, Ernst Joseph 124
Welch, John W. 30, 131
Whitaker, Richard 31, 114, 115
White, John L. 113, 114, 121
White, Leland J. 21
Wiles, G. P. 134, 136
Wills, Garry 25, 111
Wilson, John R. 129
Woodman, Tony 17, 18, 110-11
Wuellner, Wilhelm 46, 121, 130, 131, 136
Yarbrough, O. Larry 32, 85
Zarefsky, David 136
Ziolkowski, John 122

BIBLICAL REFERENCES

Job
8:3-4 136

1 Maccabees
6:12-13 126

4 Maccabees
1:1, 3 118
2:2-3 118

Acts
5 126
2:44-47 129
4:32-37 129
12:19-23 126
17 94-95
17:4 117
18:3 38

Romans
7 110
7:19 20

1 Corinthians
4:12 38
5, 6 45
8:1-11:1 120
9 120

2 Corinthians
8 22, 96
8:2-4 22, 94-95

Philippians
4:1, 9; 5:1 114

1 Thessalonians
1:1 56, 74, 104, 129
1:1 69-70, 73-75
1:1-5 67, 69-70, 75, 79, 131
1:1-10 131
1:1-2:12 36
1:2 56, 58, 74, 78, 128, 131, 133

1:2-4 69-70, 75
1:2-10 131
1:3 39, 56, 70, 74, 104, 129, 131
1:4 56, 70, 72, 104, 131
1:5 69-72, 75, 132
1:5-9 129
1:6 55, 72, 76-77, 99, 132
1:6-10 36, 77-88, 80
1:6-2:16 67, 75-80
1:7 56, 83, 79
1:7-10 77
1:8 28, 64, 72, 83
1:9 27, 46, 52, 54, 63-64, 72, 99, 117
1:10 27, 46, 52, 56, 64, 74, 77, 104, 129
2:1 81, 104 , 132
2:1-2 77, 78
2:1-12 32, 36, 37-39, 55, 64-65, 72, 76-80, 83-84, 87, 116, 118, 121
2:2 27, 78, 132
2:3-4 78
2:3-5 38
2:3-12 133
2:4 38, 71, 83, 99, 127
2:5 36, 39, 132
2:5-8 78
2:6 39, 79
2:7 79, 103, 118, 129, 138
2:8 36, 129
2:9 38, 83, 104, 132
2:9-12 22, 38, 78-79, 94, 119
2:10 132

2:11 36, 83, 129, 132
2:12 39, 56, 78, 84-87, 99, 103, 105, 129, 133
2:13 36, 39, 46, 52, 58, 72, 77, 132-133
2:13-16 36, 62, 67, 77-78, 80, 85, 99, 117, 132
2:14 54-55, 64, 72-74, 76, 104, 108,130
2:14-15 55
2:14-16 35-36, 66, 77, 125
2:15 77, 99, 108
2:16 56, 73, 77, 108
2:17 54, 57, 64, 75, 77, 82, 104
2:17-18 81
2:17-20 80-83, 134
2:17-3:13 54, 67, 75, 80-83
2:18 49, 54, 59, 66
2:19 39, 57, 66, 82, 89, 128, 134
2:20 66, 81, 99, 134
3:1-4 134
3:1-5 81
3:1-6 52
3:1-8 80, 83
3:2 39, 49, 57, 72, 83, 104
3:3 59, 126
3:3-4 81, 126
3:4 55

3:5 39, 60, 71, 73, 81
3:6 46, 49, 52, 54, 81, 83
3:6-8 51
3:7 49, 81, 83, 104
3:7-9 58
3:9 74, 82, 128, 134
3:9-13 67, 80, 81-84, 114, 134
3:10 54, 73, 82, 134
3:11 49, 54, 74, 104, 129
3:11-13 64, 74, 134
3:12 67, 86
3:13 56-57, 66, 72, 74, 82-83, 99, 104, 129
3:18 73
4 30, 65
4:1 82-84, 99, 104, 134-35
4:1-2 85
4:1-8 32, 85
4:1-12 56, 84-86, 90, 134
4:1-5:22 67, 75, 82, 84-91
4:1-5:24 134
4:2 84
4:3 85, 129
4:3-8 134
4:4 129
4:4-6a 85
4:5 35, 125
4:6 84, 134
4:6b-8 85
4:9 56, 83-86, 104, 130, 135
4:9-12 64, 73, 84-86, 100, 129, 136, 138

1 Thess. (cont.)
4:10 82-86, 104
4:11 38, 39-40, 84, 101
4:12 55, 82, 85-86, 129
4:13 53, 57, 77, 83, 89, 104, 129, 138
4:13-18 51, 59, 87-90, 135
4:13-5:11 84, 87-90
4:14 89
4:14-18 88
4:15, 16 57
4:15-17 30, 87

4:16-18 85
4:17 19, 89
4:18 73, 82, 84, 87, 125, 130
5 30, 65
5:1 104, 128, 135
5:1-11 87, 90
5:3 60, 64, 87, 90, 126, 132
5:4 60, 104, 138
5:5 74, 104,124
5:5-10 60
5:6, 8 58
5:9 27, 56, 90
5:9-10 87, 90
5:11 58, 73, 82-84, 86-87,

125, 130
5:12 72, 104
5:12-13 39
5:12-15 82, 84,86
5:12-22 84, 86-87, 90, 114, 135
5:12-24 134
5:13 39, 130
5:14 55, 84, 104, 123
5:16 128
5:16-22 87
5:17 128
5:18 58, 74, 133
5:21 87, 135
5:22 134-136
5:23 74, 91, 92,

134, 136
5:23-24 91, 134
5:23-28 67, 91-92, 136, 138
5:24 56, 74, 91-92, 100, 134, 136
5:25 91, 104
5:25-28 91
5:26 63, 91, 104
5:27 30, 91, 104
5:28 91, 92

2 Thessalonians
3:6 94, 110
3:6-12 119
3:11-12 135

ANCIENT AUTHORS

Ad Herennium
1.5.1 131
1.8 75
2.30.47-31.50 131,136
3.8.15 116, 120
4.2-4 115
4.15.21 68
4.17.24 114
4.20.27 68
4.26.36 135
4.27.37 69
4.35 31
4.42.54-56 114
4.45.59-48.61 115
4.49.68 31
5.8 131

Aelius
Theon
3.251 116

Aphthenius
32.27 34

Aristotle
Rhetoric
1.1.15 29

1.2.4 32
1.3.1 120
2.1.5 116
2.13.16 71
2.20.2 115
2.21 114
2.21.2, 16 121
3.7.7 121
3.13.12 69-70
3.13.14 70
3.14.7 70
3.16.11 116, 120

Problems
18.3 31

Chariton
Chaereas and
Callirhoe
3.6.8 63, 124
3.7.3 129
4.2.14 63, 129
4.4.1 63, 124
5.2.6 63, 124
7.1.7 63
8.1.6 124
8.8.12 63, 129

Cicero
Academica
2.135 122

De Legibus
2.4 116

Pro Flacco
18 37

De Officiis
1.42 37

Tusculan
Disputations
1.112-17 50
3.13 122
3.23.55 81, 128
3.34 122
3.34.81 53
3.81 88
4.38 122
4.63 55

Ad Brutum
2.2 53
1.9 80

Ad Familiares
1.3.1 54
5.16 80, 123, 124
5.16.5 134
6.3 80

De Inventione
1-57 121
1.5.7 116
1.15.20 70
1.16.22 131
1.22.31 134
1.30.49 115
1.47 63, 71, 118
1.51.97 114
1.52 136
1.53-56 131
2.52.157 116, 121
2.77.311-12 114

De Partitione
Oratoria
27.97 70

De Oratore
2.19.80 114, 136
3.53.203 114
34.122 131

Cicero (cont.)
50.168 113
63.212 114

Topica
10.41-45 115

Demetrius
Elocution
(On Style)
202 30
223 113

Dio Chrysostom
Orations
4.28-39 131
8.8 122
24.3 28
27.8-9 48
48.10 37

Diodorus
Library of History
35.2.47 126

Diogenes Laertius
Vita (Lives of Emi-
nent Philosophers)
2.82 119
4.128 119
6.2 119
118 81

Dionysius of
Halicarnassus
Demosthenes
48 114

On Word
Arrangement
3 114

Roman Antiquities
11.28-29 118, 133

Epictetus
Discourses
1.29.46.47 126

2.139 126
3.22.56 126
3.22.57 78
3.24.103-4 128
4.1.176 126
4.8.30-32 126
4.10.10 78

Hermogenes
On Invention
4.2 30
9.24 34
46-49 116

Homer
The Iliad
24.549-51 122

The Odyssey
1.345-355 122

Isocrates
Evagoras
77 116

Josephus
Antiquities
1.15.91 118
19.8.2 126

Jewish War
194 49

Juvenal
Satire
13 53

Libanius
Progymnasmata
349-360 119

Livy
3.44-48 118, 133
40, 37, 2 136

Longinus
Sublime
40.2 114

Lucian
De Conscribenda
Historia
55 68

Lucretius
De Rerum Natura
783 122

Menander
Dyskolos
1.28 37
2.487-498 37
2.682-85 37

Menander
Rhetores
413.5-414.30 124
413.5-414.810
122

Ovid
Tristia
1.3 54
1.8.11 63, 124

Pontiques
3.5.37-38 63, 124

Philo
Cherubim
17.4 118

De Vita Mosis
2.209-216 131

Special Laws
1.300, 309, 318
132

Plato
Phaedrus
217B 44
261A 29

Republic
10.603-4 130

Pliny the Elder
Epistles
5.16.3 133
6.3 133
6.3, 5.16.3 118
9.30.1 63
9.33 30

Plutarch
A Pleasant Life
Impossible
1105E 57

Consolatio
ad Uxorem
608B 75
608F 132
608F-610C 76,
125
609D 57, 132
610C 135
610D 135
611 57, 135
611A 128
611C 89

Consolatio ad
Apollonium
102A 75
102B 121-123
103A 135
106B-C 54, 55
107D 127
111B 56, 135
111C-D 136
113A 103
113C 88-89
116E 54
117B 136
117F 125, 133
119D 54, 60, 132,
135
119E 56, 135
120B 127

De Amicorum
Multitudine
95A 129

Plutarch (cont.)
96A 57, 63, 129
96B 63, 129
96D 57, 129

Education
of Children
7F 118

Lives
4.5 119

Moralia
48E-74E 118
169D 116
1033B-1057C 116
1086C-1107C 116
814C 63

On Exile
599B 49
605B 127

Pseudo-Ovid
Ad Liviam
209-216 127

Pseudo-Phocylides
194 118

Quintilian
Institutio Oratoria
2.4.24 119
3.4.6-16 116, 121
3.7.10-11 33
3.8.6, 10 70
3.8.59 69
4.2.83-84 29
4.3.14 114
4.5.22-24 69
4.11.6 115
5.8 67
5.10.41 116
5.11.5-16 115

5.11.6 31
5.22 27
8.3.83 110
8.5.3 114
9.1.30 69, 135
9.2.47 69
9.3.99 119

Qumran
1QM 125
1QS 2.16-17 64
1QS 9.16-18 64
1QH 2.23-25 130
1QH 4.13-14 64

Rhetorica ad
Alexandrum
34 131, 136
36.15-22 131, 136

Seneca
Ad Marciam
1.1 103
1.1-4 131
1.2 75
1.2-4 50
1.3-5.6 50
1.5 65
1.5-1.8 132
1.7 50
1.19 127, 133,
   134
2.1 124
2.3 125
4.3 125
5.5-6 135
5.16 127
7.1 65, 130
9.1 65
15.1 125
15.2 125
16.1 56, 103, 135
22.3 126
22.5-6 50

Ad Helviam
1 75
1.1 131
2.1-2.4 76
2.5 75
3.2 103
4.1 133
5.1 135
5.3 58, 60
5.5 56, 135
5.5-6 56
10.4 119
10.7 119
10.8 119
14.2 103
17.5 58
18.5-19.4 129
18.7 124

Ad Polybium
6.1-2 103
7.11 129
14-16.3 80
17.1, 2, 6 132
18.1 58

Const. Sap.
19.3 58

Epistles
6.3-5 115
6.4 115
6.5 115
9.8.8 63
13.1 127
13.1-3 56, 135
17 53
18.6 58
22.1 116
24.15 128
27.1 116
29.4 116
40.5 116
48.2-4 63

50.4 116
52.2 116
52.7 116
52.8 116
63 123
64.8 116
72.5-6 116
94.24 116
95.29 116
91.4 128
93 123
99 123
100.12 116

Ira
2.10.7 122

On Benefits
1.10 137

Providentia
1.4 126
1.5 126
2.6 126
4.16 127

De Vita Beata
26.2 58

Sibylline Oracles
3.34-35.601-34
   125

Tacitus
Annals
6.47 125

Virgil
Aeneid
1-6 126
6.785-88 112